FORTUNATE SON

★ HIGH ROAD BOOKS An Imprint of the University of New Mexico Press Albuquerque

RICK BASS

FORTUNATE SON

selected essays
from the
lone star state

HIGH
ROAD

High Road Books is an imprint
of the University of New Mexico Press

ISBN 978-0-8263-6245-2 (paper)
ISBN 978-0-8263-6246-9 (electronic)

Library of Congress Control Number: 2020949862

Cover photograph by Jay Sauceda
Designed by Mindy Basinger Hill
Composed in Garamond Premier Pro and Sutro Deluxe

CONTENTS

5/12/20

Dear Richard,

I have finished my critique of your Texas stories. Overall I really am proud of the maturity your writing has evolved. Very few people floating under the ice downstream.

I missed 5, 6, 7, 8. In progress? Lots of adventures of Kirby. Careful about specific comments about politics in a book of ENTERTAINMENT. Let politics be politics AND Adventures be adventures. I Like your characters. I made notes as I went along. hmmm Gave a lot of thought to the "ugly thing"

hmmmm

★

FOR MY FATHER AND MOTHER,
Charles R. Bass and Mary Lucy Robson Bass

AND MY BROTHERS,
Frank Robson and William James

INTRODUCTION

WHAT MAKES A TEXAN? The idea has been explored exhaustively; to even ask the question implies a cultural self-awareness that is perhaps prideful and parochial. I'm not old yet, but my grandmothers, born in 1898 and 1906, are starting to get near the territory of old—123 and 115 years old this spring and summer, were they still alive.

They have not been gone all that long.

The conversations and stories they shared with me when I was a child, about the old days, and the stories that old people had shared with them when my grandmothers were young children. . . . Well, you get the picture.

Would they have said that Texas had changed in their own lifetime? Surely. Might they have said there *was* no more Texas? I do not think so. And yet here I am, musing that this may be the case.

Things don't go away, right? They just . . . change.

Maybe this questioning has to do with my exile: Utah, Arkansas, Mississippi, and finally—an uphill version of the angle of repose—Montana. For the last thirty-four years, I've lived in a tiny valley in Montana, as far from the Texas border country as I could get: the Canadian border.

I chose a place where there was more space and, in the bounty of public land, fewer boundaries and fences. As if I had been told, as a child, such places existed.

I left when I was eighteen. Did I leave? If I keep coming back, it can't be said that I have left, can it? Only that I have expanded the arc and loop of my orbit. Now maybe I'm 97 percent Montana, 3 percent Texas, at the surface, but within, I still carry fiercely those same elements I was born with. Through the decades, and tens of thousands of miles of crawling through the jungled forests, breathing the fire smoke, drinking the lake and creek water, eating the elk, and sleeping beneath the net of Montana's particular stars has transformed me—but still, within me, there remain crystals of where I came from, and that which will be in me always.

I remember when I first moved to Montana. I was caretaking a drafty, cavernous hunting lodge with no heat source save for the giant stone fireplace downstairs, large enough in which to roast a pig, which I regret now I never did. (My deer-hunting grandfather, an inveterate eater of pork, used to say "I never see a pig, I don't tip my hat.") The only place I could find warmth during the long winters was in the greenhouse, where the overhead plastic sheeting gathered what wan gray winter light sifted down from the scudding, bruise-colored clouds that enveloped the valley from November until March, siftings of dull light wiggling in cartoon fashion through the opaque roof and falling upon the wilted, brittle-stick skeletons of tomato plants and the black soil. It wasn't warmth, but it was something, and I breathed it: the ghost of hope, the echo of life.

There was a tiny barrel stove at the end of it and a rickety table that shook whenever I got to writing too fast. A stove lid was cut into the top of the barrel and when the splints of pine kindling I shoved into this tiny furnace burned hottest, there was a great roar from within, and the little lid rattled almost musically; and with my gloved hand (rag wool, but with the fingers cut off so I could hold the pen), I would write as fast as I could, as if trying to keep up with the tempo of warmth. Remembering Texas, and Mississippi, where I lived for some years after college—but not missing it.

There were many mornings I had to warm the pen on the stove before the ink would come out.

The fire burned at different tempos; I didn't always keep it roaring. The greenhouse warmed slowly—a giant clock-faced analog thermometer pegged 40, then 45 degrees, each morning, no matter the subzero depths outside—and as the inferno quieted to a more sustained murmuring, I found that so too was my glide down into the dreamland of my story facilitated by the acoustics of warmth, and of survival.

The year was 1987, then '88, then '89. It occurs to me that one of the more fascinating characteristics of history is how sometimes one doesn't recognize it as history. It was the time of the timber wars in Montana, in which I was actively engaged, but I didn't recognize it as a historical period; to me, it was just life. Each morning, before my activism, I leaned into story-writing, and for a little while, I forgot about much else.

There are of course exceptions to one's lack of awareness regarding the intrusions of history. In Houston, my mother coming in my room at 6509 Neff Street (where in my closet I stabled imaginary Pegasus) and telling me the president had been shot. The first time I ever saw her cry. Until then, I did not know adults could do that.

The *Gore v. Bush* recount; I was home for that one too. Visiting the state capitol in Austin, a Texas hill country pink granite perfect replica of the nation's capitol, for a book festival, I walked hand in hand with my daughters, past protestors who were chanting, *What do we want? Democracy! When do we want it? Now!*—a catchy sing-song tune that stayed with the girls for years afterward.

Stories, like lives, can and do change as they travel through the world, seeking a fit, adapting and metamorphosing. For better or worse, the sagas and stories of our childhood form us. As adults, it's how we modify not just ourselves but the stories that matters most. The Alamo is within me from childhood, the narrative of a small band making a stand against an outsized opponent, with everything at stake. The tale resonated with the child I was—and, even today, is, I suspect, the unsolicited source of a certain element of fiest. Later, I would come to see the ballad of the Alamo for what it was: the territorial imperative of renegade drifters, some outlaws, scofflaws, brokenhearted and antisocial. New folks drifted into territory already occupied, declared it their own, displaced and/or killed the previous residents. In some cultures this is called *war*; in others, *legend*, or *heroism*, or *valor*. I was recently repulsed to hear in the 2019 State of the Union, the then–chief executive, praise with such effusion and at such length the heroes of the Alamo—clearly trolling for electoral votes and appealing to the militia/antigovernment "Don't Tread on Me" violence-fueled base that was his rabid constituency—and in his next breath further glorifying a culture of guns and gun violence by adding to his pantheon of American heroes Wyatt Earp, Davy Crockett, and Annie Oakley, with the only commonality among them being their renown with pistols and/or rifles.

It is my Texas parochialism, in me since childhood, that tells him to keep his sorry New York developer-ass out of the Lone Star state. To rephrase Lyle Lovett, *That's right, you're not from Texas, but Texas doesn't want you anyway.*

Those Alamo days presaged by some 150 years my own westward drift, just as had one of my progenitors, Austin Gore Lowry, set out into the world on his own drift west from Tennessee to Texas. (Sitting by a smudgy fire in November, or December, or January—the chilliest months in Tennessee—did he, *could* he, ever imagine a descendant of his ever walking quietly through the old forests and snowy mountains amid the immense pawprints of grizzly bears, and serenaded by wolves, walking in a land that had no name yet, or rather, no name or country known yet to European Americans?)

It seems beyond our species' capability to imagine so many generations into the future. Certainly, I have no ability to imagine a grandchild, a great-grandchild, a great-great-grandchild. Such visioning seems as distant as, or more distant than, the firmament of our imagination.

And yet, I look back at these essays from a place in time—Texas, and my life—and realize this is not unlike what writers seek to do. We choose and select that which we wish to send forward into the reservoir of time. We select that which has beauty, rather than hoarding it in the vault of our brainpan, to vanish. Instead, we send it forward. We still cannot see who will receive it, but we send it to them, trusting it will find those with whom it will resonate—perhaps influencing their lives, shaping or reinforcing their aesthetics and values, which is to say, nurturing their character, which is to say, participating in their destiny.

That which one searches for is seeking the searcher, too.

★

As a geologist, I understand that borders are always a permeable membrane. They come and go; things change, borders contract and compress like a living entity, an organism unto itself. History breathes, wanders, moves. It is the oldest and yet most shocking truth: nothing stays the same.

No ideas but in things, wrote William Carlos Williams. Antlers, fire, stone, water, books, music, family. Which is more beautiful: the pink granite boulders of the hill country, recent extrusions from a passionate, ancient past, or the even more recent detritus of their disintegration spreading across the land in a deltaic splay of pink, with the formerly isolated crystals now released from their matrix—feldspar, zinc, mica, pyrite—but still with us, always with us?

There is no veil.

★

I want to return to this theme of metamorphosis. Concurrent with this discussion are the two governing components of our existence: space and time. My father, in his geophysical subsurface explorations, has traveled the world over countless times and followed the relatively slow speed of sound waves of energy across billions of years. At the other end of the country, I wander one particular mountain range, up and down only a few thousand feet each day, in only one point in time, *a day*: so finite a unit that for all intents it can be said to be invisible, nonexistent.

My father has always had the worldview that the universe is balanced and just-right—that for everything that is given, something is taken away. This is an old belief, observed by Indigenous people around the world.

My own ethos, that no work is ever wasted, is in parallel with my father's. Both acknowledge that our world—whether in Montana or Texas—is a closed and finite system, with all that ever was or will be, contained within.

One of the formative ideas from my youth was taken as an article of faith from Walter Prescott Webb's *The Great Plains*. Cribbing from John Wesley Powell, Webb agreed that much of the history of the American West was and forever will be shaped by the presence or absence of water.

Other childhood stories: the aforementioned and magnificently scored (Dimitri Tiomkin) *The Alamo*.

Later, in Texas, how could poets such as Naomi Nye and novelists such as Sandra Cisneros and Sarah Bird, nonfiction writers like Willie Morris and Diane Wilson (talk about *fiest*!), or filmmakers like Wes Anderson, actors like Luke and Owen Wilson, photographers like Keith Carter, *not* emerge, when the pressure of so much sameness was being applied, pressing down on all?

There was never sameness. There was disproportion, but there was never sameness.

★

Another of the myths of my growing up in Texas was the story of excess—that Texas was a land of unlimited bounty is another narrative I have seen deconstructed by time. And even nestled amid that dominant myth, there was an inextinguishable characteristic of Texas that I noticed, and which resonated with me: its duality. It almost always was one thing, but it was also almost always that thing's opposite. It was a land of milk and honey but was also "hell on horses and women." All true. It was Old South, even East, and yet it was pioneer West. It was both. It was all.

★

I would be remiss in exploring, curating, my Texan-ness, if I did not mention Kirby, my best friend from high school and, to this day, a collaborator in pushing and challenging boundaries.

Little things add up to make a life. When Kirby and I saw a neglected horse or horses standing out in a pasture, we sometimes slipped between the strands of the barbed-wire fence and went up to them, grabbed their manes, and wriggled our way up onto them; rode them bareback, often galloping some distance before being pitched, though other times not. These were never carefully tended horses but instead woolly, burr-matted, long-ignored stock, the knock-kneed and spavined left to fend for themselves in weedy scrubland that was one of the many signatures of the creeping poverty of inattention.

We fed them carrots—we almost always carried a bag for this purpose—or fistfuls of grass or twists of weeds ripped from the other side of the gnawed-bare pastures, just beyond the horses' reach.

We were adolescents, not unlike children in a zoo. The world was a zoo, and up to that point, Texas was our world. We were not great respecters of authority. We climbed over the walls at football stadiums and played catch on the Astroturf in moonlight. We drove my father's Jeep and, later, Kirby's old Mercury, out into muddy, soupy fields—*overlanding*, we called it—as far as we could reach without bogging down, for no good reason other than to see if we could reach the other side; and when we did not, we called my father to come pull us out with a chain or tow rope.

I had a pilot's license, for God's sake. We shouldn't be here, but here we still are. Kirby is a trainer and manager now for a semipro football team in Brenham, the Texas Express. The year I turned sixty, I played tailback and special teams for them. The world is beautiful, the world is strange; it's just that sometimes the boundaries need adjusting here and there.

★

Raised on the myth that Texas was a possessor of a pioneer spirit, and that farther, wilder country lay always to the west—that the frontier of Texas had over time migrated now to the west of Texas—I chose to go to college in northern Utah, to Utah State, near the Cache National Forest, not far from the High Uintas Primitive Area.

I've been in Montana now for thirty-four years. There are no roads joining this valley, the Yaak, to its sister valley in British Columbia, the Yahk, just across the imaginary dashed line that represents the border. (Though it is not entirely imaginary; the US government sawed a stripe across the mountains, a straight-line gash, an incision visible from space, for no reason other than to delineate the boundary, it seems, to the forest itself.) I wander back and forth from America's public lands into Canada's. There are more bears than people in this valley. I like it that way.

I still get back to Texas often—my dad still lives there, in Houston. My youngest brother B.J. and his wife Karen live in Austin; my cousins Randy and Russell and Aunt Lee in Houston. But Montana's my home. It occurs to me however—and it is no less true for being a bit of a cliché—that I carry Texas with me, as I go back and forth across our northern border.

★

Politics: Barbara Jordan, the George Bushes, Jim Hightower, Sam Rayburn, Molly Ivins, LBJ (I love Robert Caro's biographies), Ann Richards, the Texas Eleven—even a less than careful reader can likely parse my politics. I believe that all art is political, not in the preaching-to-the-choir or rabble-rousing sense, but instead at the most basic level: all art is about selectivity—what to put in, what to leave out—and in choosing, the artist's tastes and values and sensibilities cannot help but be illuminated and represented. Values are the heartbeat within us, cannot be stilled. The blood knows as does the dreamland of the subconscious. The story's images and gestures, like the blood within us, know.

Not all art is partisan—I believe the best art is nonpartisan—but all art is political. Speaking one's voice, whether in quiet insinuation or bold assertion, is these days more of a political act than ever, and no matter whether in fiction or nonfiction. I've found as an artist it's often best even to try to work against my values, as if reverse-engineering—being unafraid to turn one's villains loose into the story.

The borders of your values will always bind or bound your villains; your sensibilities will be protected within the structure you create. (As old revolutionaries used to claim, the master's hammer will never be used to tear down the mansion.) If the art has the integrity of craft, the more obstacles you place between you and your truth or values, the more powerful becomes the story's movement—even if sometimes circuitous—toward your truth.

To put it another way, your faith will be tested, and from that, strengthened.

Kirby and I were devoted to the board game *Risk*, where rolls of the dice delivered one continent after another to the gambler. It was a slow-motion game predicated pretty much on world domination, where a player ended up owning entire countries large and small, and built up tiny plastic armies upon the puzzle piece–fitted outlines of each state, bordered sometimes by mountain ranges, rivers, coasts, or, other times, the relentlessly unimaginative straight edge of a ruler. And then we set about on each other, seeking to capture all our opponents' armies and nations. It was a splendid game for boys, possessing no real strategy, only a willingness to roll the dice and see what fate delivered. We must have played thousands of games, while our peers were watching *Gilligan's Island*, *The Beverly Hillbillies*, *Sanford and Son*, *All in the Family*, and *M*A*S*H*.

We learned some geography—the Ukraine, Irkutsk, Yakutsk, Madagascar, Chile, Peru, Argentina, Brazil—but even in the dreamland of play, we were following those neural pathways of dispersing, then claiming that which we'd been told was the rarest and most valuable thing: land.

★

This is a journalist's Texas scrapbook, then: a firefighting story, a music pilgrimage, a ramble in Texas's tiniest public wilderness (one of only five in the entire state). Fishing with my father and uncle on a lake that is partly in Texas and partly in Louisiana; flying around the borders of Texas—usually defined by water, a resource that will vanish in much of the state within our lifetime; hanging out at my parents' cattle farm down near Goliad; reading the work of Texans before me. A visit to deer camp; a birding jet boat journey into the mouth of the Brazos; a season spent with a semipro football team in Brenham, Texas Express.

The Texas I remember no longer exists. I can write what it used to be like a short time ago, but I cannot parse or identify it now. I can only describe where I live now, trying to hide out from conflict and war, trying to become more peaceable; and in that solitude and peace, working to make beauty.

The tendrils of the DNA helices from my Texas days are still within me. I, and the Montana landscape and culture, am metamorphosing them. The transformation to Montanan is almost complete, and I can never go back—yet I revisit Texas always.

In 1898, while pouring the foundation for the Eastland County courthouse, pranksters thought it great wit to entomb in the cement beneath the cornerstone a horned toad, with nearby Texas Christian University's mascot being the TCU Fighting Horned Frogs. Fantastic creatures. A lizard, *Phrynosoma cornutum*, not at all a toad, much less a frog. They resemble dinosaurs, perhaps more than any creature left in the world, with spiny "horns" over their eyes that can shoot blood at predators. They were *ours*, common as dirt. I never took them for granted, was always thrilled to see one; and yet, they "went away," according to the colloquialism for extinction, or near-extinction. Likewise, leopard frogs. Likewise, red wolves. Likewise . . .

When contractors tore down the Eastland County courthouse for a rebuild thirty-one years later, cracking open that cornerstone and exhuming Old Rip, he was still alive. A little wizened, but remnant.

We are each born likewise, it occurs to me. I was born between a time of wolves and no wolves. With the red wolves, as well, there was a wandering strand line of their distribution, not dissimilar from the geological sinuosity of rivers altering their courses, or the fringed shorelines of bays and estuaries transgressing and regressing according first to the tides and then to a warming world we did not yet know was warming.

One of my early memories, from the age of five or six, is of the anticipation, each Sunday on the way to church, when my family would pass by "Wolf Corner," out near the Harris County line, where ranchers still trapped and shot the last red wolves found roaming the Katy Prairie. The wolves' thick-maned bodies hung draped over barbed wire like desperadoes, or like women's fine fur coats on a hanger, and I thought I understood even as a child, or perhaps particularly as a child, the fear that must have been roused in the ranchers for them to kill so beautiful an animal.

As I grew older, it became rarer to see such "bounty" posted, until finally one day the last of the wolves "went away," and then the ranchers went away, and the cattle, too, so that all was as if for naught, save for my weekly memories of the accruing loss; and gone, too, eventually, was even the church.

★

What would I place in my own time capsule? A set of steel-wheeled roller skates, a slide rule, a baseball card of the Houston Astros' Jimmy Wynn, aka The Toy Cannon. Glittery scales from an alligator gar, a bronzed prehistoric top-water fish, six feet long, like a tarpon, that cruised the sluggish bayous back then. I don't live there anymore and haven't for a long time, but it's where I come from.

I'd let the sands and sediments of time flow in and over and around my little museum of the past. Rather than sending the time capsule on a moon launch into the future, or even placing a wave-tossed message in a bottle, I'd bury it, as we tend to do with any treasure.

These essays have for me that time-capsule quality—not particularly or exclusively Texan, though the idea of time capsules does strike me as a sweet echo of the NASA culture of my youth. Even the best writing is never quite the equal of the best living; but neither are the two necessarily oppositional, which, as a young writer, I once feared they might be.

Writing is called art for a reason. It takes great artifice to capture the gestures that seem to breathe a thing into life. I'm asked sometimes if I would be a different writer if I'd grown up somewhere else other than Texas, or if I'd even be a writer at all. *Yes* to the first question, *Maybe not* to the second. Perhaps instead I'd be an environmental activist, a football coach, a firefighter, a bird-dog trainer. Maybe I'd be a geologist, a teacher, a wildlife biologist, a hunting guide, a pilot. I do believe the world tries to put all things—ultimately—where they most desire to be.

Staying there is another matter. Whirl is indeed king.

★

I was fortunate to grow up in a household that valued education, my mother teaching and then working with Cub Scouts as—how quaint yet wonderful the phrasing—a den mother. I was fortunate to receive a public education before being released into the mountains to continue my lessons at a state university, Utah State. I was fortunate both my parents valued reading and storytelling and above all encouraged time spent out-of-doors, not in structured form, nor even in a let's-visit-a national-park way. (Texas's paucity with regard to public land may yet prove to be our Achilles' heel to the whole experiment—for if there is no pride of ownership, how can we all really pull together for the preservation of a nature we've never known?)

I was fortunate to be insinuated into the earth between formal wars, after WWII and Korea but before Vietnam—though as is so often the case in these matters, there were other wars building, in which the shooting and other violence was not yet being acknowledged—and with the greatest war, the revolt of the earth against our very presence on it, and our treatment of it, being made manifest daily now.

I was fortunate, also, to be able to become, like my mother, a teacher myself. I was fortunate to grow up the son not just of a schoolteacher, but also of a geologist, an earth diver, and to become one myself.

For a long time, you are where you come from, and to be but two generations removed from the Spindletop boom—to grow up in the company of geologists who themselves had grown up in the company of those who'd inhabited those wild times, and to be a child in Houston also during the height of moonshot fever— surely impressed me with certain sensibilities, which, no matter how many hours or days or years I spend gazing out at a serene marsh in Montana, still thrum within me.

In all ways, I was born a fortunate son.

FORTUNATE SON

INTO THE FIRE

I'M RUNNING THROUGH A FIELD with my best friend, a man I went to high school with. We're on the outskirts of Houston, it's nighttime, and we can see the fire in the distance. It's a hay barn at the far end of a field that's caught fire, and the barn is burning, as are the bales of hay in it, as well as the loose bales out in the field, as is also the field stubble itself. The groves of trees at the back edge of the field are burning, too. My friend, Kirby, is a volunteer fireman now for the little community of Spring, Texas, which is a pretty suburban enclave (not that long ago, woods) nestled amid and among the concrete and chaos of Houston. Kirby is fully dressed in his turnout gear—his firefighting equipment—as am I, in a borrowed suit; I just happened to be hanging out in the station when the call came, and there was an extra set.

We have to run across a golf course, a driving range actually, to get to the fire—another station is already there; we can see the red-and-blue lights—and as we run huffing through the humid night there are little piss-ant golf balls like mushrooms everywhere, which we keep stumbling on. It seems like it's a mile to that fire and as if the whole western horizon is ablaze. The turnout gear—helmet, big-ass boots, scuba tank, bunker coat, rubber overalls, mongo gloves—feels like it weighs about seventy pounds. It feels like we'll never get there, or that if we do, we'll be too tired to fight the fire, and we'll just have to stand there gasping and sucking air at the edge of the fire, legs and lungs aflame. Probably when we were eighteen we could have just cruised on out there in forty seconds flat, never even breaking a sweat, but twenty years ago we of course would have been more interested in breaking apart order and structure than trying to weave it back together, or keep it from burning down.

Now we are finally drawing closer to the mega-fire. We're drenched with sweat inside our heavy rubber boots, and we've divoted the hell out of that golf course, tromped its sand traps, so that in daylight it will probably look like a herd of wild horses ran through. With the flames' backlighting we can see the stick figures of other firefighters moving in and through and among the flames, working with shovels and axes and hoses. There's smoke and steam, and at night like that it looks like an evacuating village, looks primitive and tribal. It seems to be calling us.

There are a lot of firefighters on this one. The barn was a goner a long time ago; the trees are goners, flames searching for the sky, but they have nowhere else to go, nothing else to burn—a city of concrete lies beyond them, with fire hydrants on every corner— and the scent of the burning hay bales and of the burning stubble smells good.

The fire's been going a pretty good while—maybe an hour, before we received our call to come help close it out. It's December, nearing Christmas and New Year's—prime time for firefighters, along with, of course, the Fourth of July and Halloween, all those candles and burning pumpkins!—and what started this fire was probably either someone trying to collect the insurance money, or a homeless person just trying to find a place to hang out and stay warm. Maybe they built a little fire with which to make coffee. Maybe a cigarette fell in the hay. Either of these two explanations is just as likely; or it could have been kids—eighteen years old, perhaps—just out fucking around. In December like this, it was almost certainly a human-caused fire, some errant excess of social imbalance, some fringe unraveling or deterioration, and now the firefighters are here to snip off that excess and snuff it out and smooth it over. It may seem like a cliché, and you may, when the talk turns to firefighters, and especially volunteers, hear the easy stereotype, the armchair assumption of "hero complex" or "boring home life—needs excitement."

It's not this way at all. Perhaps for a handful of them it is that way, but far more common I think are the ones who do it for the same reasons that any of us do whatever it is we do, or dream of doing: the act of it achieves a fit and an order with the rhythms and essence within. You run across fields with them, you race around town with them from call to call, and pretty soon you realize it's just the way they are. You start to view them not as individuals but as a force, summoned and directed by nature, like the fire itself; that in a world with fire, there must also exist a force that desires for fires to be put out—and that further, the two forces desire and require each other.

They love to put out the fires, as does, perhaps, a rainstorm. Plus, when it's not dangerous, it's fun. It tips the world a bit sideways—reorders it, makes it new, re-charges it. At this particular fire everyone is sweating like racehorses and walking around ankle deep in smoldering smoke and flames and ashes and coals, some of us wearing masks and helmets, others of us bare-faced for a moment in the night air, breathing good cold air and the sweet odor of dry burning grass. We are pawing at the smoking, burning ground with rakes and shovels, breaking apart the hay bales so they will finish burning and we can go home (they flame brightly, like marshmallows, each time we separate a sheaf of them). And because I do not want to upset the rhythm of things—despite the presence of several units, several stations, they all are more or less familiar with each other, by sight if not name, as would be athletes who trained or competed together, though in this case they have risked their lives together, each time they assemble—I keep my Darth Vader mask on. There must be thirty of us out there, wandering through the night and the flames, each one of us looking

3

to me like any of the others; but they can tell, I know, when I pass near them that I am not of them, and I duck my head and turn my shoulders when I see one of the various captains or commanders, whose job it is in instances like these not to fight the fire hand to hand, but to deploy his or her men and observe, like a hawk from above, the flow of things—the comings and goings. To these men I stand out like the proverbial sore thumb, and though I have permission to be hanging out with Kirby (who is also a captain), I try to steer clear of the men and women who are carrying radios; I try not to interrupt the pulse and rhythm of the thing they have become, in their assemblage, which is a force that is hopefully equal to that of the fire. We hear the phrases "armed forces" and "show of force," but the way I mean it, *force* is more elemental than that. I mean it like rain or wind or desire; like gravity or oxygen.

I can feel them scowling after me as I career away from the ones-with-radios. I strike at the smoldering hay bales, break them apart and rake them flat, soothing order back into the system. I had hoped that in theory everyone would think I was a rookie with another captain's department, one they had not seen in action yet. But of course it did not work out that way: they could all sense or see that I was different, not of them, as if a deer were trying to walk among a gathering of bears, or a moose through a flock of geese, even at night, and even amid smoke and flame. I was not an element of their force.

Kirby, picking up on the vibes that are gathering around me—the way my presence is confusing and annoying the various captains—escorts me to the perimeter of the fire, to a still-smol-dering section of field that has pretty much already been mopped up. There are puddles of water standing here and there. We walk past the incredible sight of two beautiful red-haired women sit-ting side by side on a bale of hay that is still burning. They are resting, their turnout coats opened to their T-shirts, and as the firelight flickers on their faces—red freckles, copper skin—it seems they could be drinking a cup of coffee and talking about any old thing, rather than resting, grimy and damp, having kicked this fire's ass—having sewn order back into being.

It inflames the senses. It—firefighting—argues against chaos, even while at the same time celebrating and marveling at our proximity to it. From a distance it just looks like a bunch of men and, increasingly, women, running around trying to react against and defend something. It looks a little ragged, a little mechanical. From the outside, you don't quite understand that even as you watch the men and women swirl about (dragging hose, swinging ax), a transmutation is occurring; that they are altering themselves from individuals into connected components often equal or superior to the force of the fire itself. You can't really see or feel the magic unless you are right in with them—as if in, perhaps, the eye of a hurricane. From a distance, to you, it looks as if they are running behind, playing catch-up, and that the fire is in control.

You'd never guess that the opposite is true: that they are in control, and not behind, but in lock-step with it, feeding on its energy; that the fire is the thing that allows them to exist, and as it releases stored energy in the burning, it makes that much more energy available to them for them to bend and shape and alter and turn and compress and redirect.

You need to go right into the center of the fire to see this.

★

Going into the fire of course is the worst thing in the world you can do, the last thing you should ever consider doing. The absolute best thing civilians can do is to melt and disappear, to draw way back—to become invisible, if possible, and let the two forces sweep in against each other. This is hard to do. We each have in us an innate longing for spectacle and drama, for an arousal of the senses—as wire desires electricity, as wood desires rot or flame—and when the trucks race past, or the smoke billows from the building across the street, we are drawn to it like angels, or moths. We gather, we get in the way, we clog things up. There is something Godlike in the way they hurl themselves at the fire and shut it down cold—something monstrous, too—and wherever they go, people are following behind them, clinging to the charred edges of the event, gawking and getting too close to the hoses and the crumbling, crashing-down walls of things, so that the firefighters can hardly ever concentrate purely on the task at hand, aligning their undiluted force squarely against that of the onrushing fire. Always, it seems, they are anxious to make that leap from humans to godlikes, forgetting about the people behind them—the spectators, the traffic—and hurling themselves instead completely into the matching of the fire's force. But always, it seems, there is energy that must be expended by them, wasteful energy, patrolling their flanks, and keeping humans from edging too close, or even following, again like moths.

I often wonder where such men and women come from. It—firefighting—is both an art and a science. It remakes the individual. In the instance of my best friend, Kirby, it is a marvel to see. This is not the place for such stories, but suffice it to say that twenty years ago he, we, were masters of—what? Shall we call it unraveling things, and pause there? (Fire was not involved, but might as well have been.)

The fires have transformed him—they have found him and summoned and recast him. I do not know why. It is tempting to think that for each of these firefighters there is some space within them waiting to be ignited when the fire, or the beckons, sweeps over them—and that either you have this place in you or you do not.

I think this is how it is. Plenty of people have hidden or buried or held deep within them the desire for order, sometimes extreme order, just as plenty of them have the opposite desire. There are also plenty with a desire for beauty, and no small number who are enraptured these days with the stupid, the insipid, the untruthful, and the plain plug-ugly.

But it is not that simple. There are only handfuls of them here and there who love to wade into fire and if you ask them, not a damn one of them, not even Kirby, can tell you exactly or even satisfactorily why they do it. And in observing them one of the things you pick up on pretty quick, if you're in close enough, is that, unlike many other things, there seems not to be so much a joy or a pleasure in the doing (if anything, they appear to be in a zone of near-hypnotic trance), but rather a deep sweetness of relief and fullness in the *after* of it. The pleasure of pulling off dirty turnout gear, dirty boots. Looking forward to a cleansing shower.

It's not very Zen. Or maybe it's real Zen. But I don't think so.

★

Sometimes one fire—the excitement of it, the sensation of it—will seemingly ignite other fires in the same area, days and even weeks or months later, like some kind of delayed fuse. Even if the first one was accidental, non-arson in nature, something will often have been released—something latent—in a handful of individuals within that community. And, pining and lonesome for the return of that kind of excitement, hungry to have the senses felt that deeply again (and cherishing perhaps, too—though we can only guess—the relief of the aftermath, as the throbbing senses cool and return to normal), that individual, or individuals, will set a fire, seeking to lure or beckon the firemen's return.

And always, they come. Occasionally it will be one of the firemen themselves who has set the fire—the bad seed getting in among them and somehow confused, seeking to simultaneously create and destroy the very thing that gives them purpose, the thing that calls, shapes, and alters them—yet seeking, in a kind of gluttony, to elude or short-cut the rules.

But the men and women in the fire departments are extraordinarily good at sniffing out this kind of firefighter: of determining, as if with ESP, when such a hybrid or renegade is in their midst. They sense it perhaps as the magma flow of a volcano senses the presence within it of a floating chunk of boulder—that which has not yet completely given itself over to the rest. They sense it, by and by—soon enough—when they are fighting fire, side by side, with such an individual, and they can sense it coming from him or her when they are back at the station watching a football game on the television. They can feel it and hear it and see it coming off him or her in waves, as if that individual in their midst is not at peace but aflame, or at least smoldering. They can sense soon enough, by the way he does not fit the rhythm that is their force, that he or she is the one who is setting the fires in order to be drawn to them and engaged by them; and because this goes against the code of ethics, and the code of physics—the law of nature that lets them and the fires exist in the same universe—they turn him or her in, or drum him or her out. They can sense it, suddenly—can see it—as if the message is writing itself in some awful hieroglyphics across the perpetrator's body.

It is elemental, the way they find out. It is the way animals communicate—the way animals, who have been here in the world so much longer than we, communicate. They are never wrong.

It is as if their existence, their integrity—the purity of their desire and being—has been threatened near unto extinction, by the presence of one such among them, and it is as if that one has willfully been gambling their lives, rolling the dice, oblivious to the risk that's being run: the threat of this stranger among them putting their life on the line for mere joy or pleasure—risking a child's father, a woman's husband, a mother's son, or a husband's wife. Rolling the dice.

There was one firefighter like this that Kirby found out about—not in his department, but in a nearby unit. Such is the hatred among the fraternity, or family, of firefighters that even he, my best friend, cannot, or will not, speak to me of him. His voice deepens and his words thicken with rage and wonder; he shakes his head *no*, never mind . . . It strikes me that it, the firebug among them, is like the metaphor, or transformation from metaphor to reality, of their fear, their foe—a building, a structure of integrity and order—burning from within.

It's rare. Much more common are the grass fires, electrical fires, and cookfires out of control; the propane heater fires, the careless-with-matches fires, the industrial fires, chemical fires, fires started by the friction of two dry branches rubbing together, fires started by lightning, fires started by oily rags, by fireworks, by hot mufflers, by magnifying glasses, by cigarettes. People fall asleep smoking in bed and immolate themselves by the dozens, even hundreds, each year. Sometimes they do it in high-rise hotels and take out dozens or hundreds with them in a single night. Archaeologists excavating the ruined cities of the future might mistakenly believe, viewing the remains, that fire still played an important part in the culture or religion of these times: that sacrifices were still common, and that at any given time, in these ghost cities, there would have been fires raging, consuming.

But they would not in their archaeological diggings be able to catch the sound of the fire engines racing toward those fires; would not be able to measure the sweat and fury and muscle-cost of the firefighters tending the water-taut hose lines, and swinging axes, shouting instructions: the tension and determination and purity-of-focus as tight as the fire was loose and raging.

Things being cast anew, or tautened and strengthened, by the fires—the archaeologists would miss that. The order which the firefighters cannot restore in the fires' consumption gets instead, sometimes, turned within them, as if with an overflowing, or excess. They come to rely (and be incorporated by) lists and repetition. They can enumerate danger better than anyone—have observed and learned the vertical and horizontal components of it (as if it is thick, like nests of snakes or hives of bees) behind the walls of things, and just beneath the skin of the earth, waiting to be peeled back or released by a simple nick or a cut. Their minds are wire-taut with understandings of possibility and cause-and-effect. They break down the world into three components: fuel, oxygen, and heat.

When they relax, they do so deeply. Their family lives, rather than becoming weakened by the attention to and obsession with fire, and the time spent at the station, often instead become strengthened. The weave and rhythm of their profession becomes similarly the fabric of their other family, their blood family. You will notice in most of them a celebration of order and structure. They're big on picnics and cookouts, circuses, trips to the beach, parades, rodeos, trips to the zoo—that kind of thing. They have a ferocity for life, even in the midst of what can be a physically and intellectually desensitizing, unstimulating environment: the late twentieth-century suburban landscape, and beyond that, the decaying cores of the urban interior.

They tend to be aware, too, of how thin the crust or skin of the earth is. Nick it and fire issues forth, is how it must seem to them. Generalizations are easy and hence dangerous, but I could not help noticing that the "thinkers" (the captains and lieutenants) often tend to be, if not fundamentally, at least peripherally religious—stolid to near-stolid churchgoers—while the more physically responsive firefighters (the ones who are not so much interested in plotting or strategizing but instead like to hurl themselves at and against the fire according to the captain's or lieutenant's directions) are usually reckless to an extreme, living what might be called a compromising or high-risk lifestyle: drinking hard, smoking hard, driving fast; acknowledging the nearness of death and disorder, by their actions, every bit as much as the churchgoers.

Hanging out with a firefighter, you learn to see the city not as some artificial and completely controlled system, but as an organism: as a pulsing, supple, almost living thing, responsive to the world. Sometimes things in a city burn because they are meant to, and need to—rotting timbers, rat-chewed wiring systems—and other times, as with the cases of arson, the fires pop up in what seems an illogical response, like cancer, done purposely and malignantly to harm the good cells surrounding a body and bring them to ruin.

It's amazing how much of a good-sized city is burning at any one time, and even more amazing how much of a city has burned, cumulatively, in the past—as if the scars of fire overlay every inch of the earth, rural or urban, several layers deep; as if the skin of the earth is burning daily, a necessary way of replenishing and invigorating itself, as our own cells are said to do every two or three days.

Riding around the city with Kirby I was almost disbelieving as he pointed out various structures that had burned. I thought it was a joke at first, a parody of a firefighter's view of his or her city, but it was actually the way he saw it. As if with the X-ray vision of history, he seemed to look right through the glossy surface, the skin, of new paint jobs and newly constructed exteriors and still see hidden within those structures the ghosts of old fires, like opponents with whom he had once done battle. It seemed that at any given point in time there would always be somewhere within the range of his vision at least one building, and usually more, where a fire had occurred during his ten years on the force. We all have our lenses for viewing the world. "How many memorable localities in a river walk!" wrote Thoreau. "Here is the warm wood side; next, the good fishing bay; and next, where the old settler was drowned when crossing on the ice a hundred years ago. It is all storied."

We all see the world through different lenses, according to our various knowledge and life experience. Doctors, farmers, writers, will look at a landscape and its inhabitants each in a way slightly different from the other, and in so doing, come up with different translations or interpretations, different perceptions, about that place. Kirby's lens is fire. There is only that which has burned in the past, or which is at risk in the future. There is also a very small portion of the world—within the range of his roving gaze—that is, for the moment, for the time being, safe, secure.

The stories with which Kirby sees his city all involve fire. We cannot drive past a place, it seems, without his having a story—as if they are latticed between the walls of structures, waiting to be released by fire, or as if the stories are the structures, like the skeletal system of a structure. Not timber and steel and stucco and concrete, but stories, with humans living within them like ants.

He was not inhumane as a teenager—no more than most—but it seems that the firefighting has made him more humane, more understanding of and attentive to the stories within the latticeworks. It's a little fascinating to me, as a writer, the way we went different directions after high school—he to marriage and children almost immediately, and to an increasingly fine and responsible job with a suit and tie and office and secretarial staff, appraising urban structures not for fire-worthiness, or fireproof-ness, but for tax assignations—while I went in what I thought was a different direction, writing stories and novels, and hanging out in the woods.

Now I am noticing that our paths did not really diverge at that significant an angle: that he sits at his desk in his day job, high above the city, and runs his evaluation sheets, his analyses, through the computer—but at night, or even in the day, when the dispatcher's horn sounds, he becomes more sensate, more alive, and he rushes to the fire eagerly. And in moving toward that fire—one after the other after the other—and in the fighting of it, he is as passionate and engaged not just with the process but with the stories and lives of the structure's inhabitants; as passionate and engaged as any writer could ever hope to be about the characters housed within his or her story, and I watch this and try to learn from it. I try to imagine all characters as inhabiting invisible or hidden stories latticeworked around them, both constraining and supporting them, which can then be released around them—the walls falling away—by fire. In ways that no writing class has yet been able to impress upon me, I begin to think about structure, about what it is, and about the forces that tug and pull at it.

I wonder what it must be like for Kirby's coworkers, to hear, in their air-conditioned offices, the squelch and bawl of his beeper down the hallway; what it must be like to see him emerge from his office like a hornet from its nest; to leave them and hurl himself out into the hot flames of Houston—hot sky, hot concrete, hot chrome, hot glass . . .

Certainly his wife, Jean Ann, has mixed feelings about it, both with regard to her and Kirby's security as well as that of their two children, and Kirby's daughter from the first marriage—her step-daughter, my goddaughter. Jean Ann knows full well that it's a big part of what makes him be alive, what makes him be Kirby, what makes him not just the man but the force she married. But she cannot help but also know full well that he is rolling some kind of dice each time he goes out the door—rolling them not just for his own senses of being alive, but to help other people in dire straits, even strangers—and it seems that she walks well a fine line between the two territories; that their marriage has a sharpness and defined clarity to it, a being-in-the-moment quality to it that may or may not be connected to the firefighting, though it is hard to imagine how it is not at least in part. It's impossible for me to watch him go briskly out the door of his home, or out of the fire station, en route, and not think of the Neil Young line—"The same thing that makes you live will kill you in the end"—just as it is impossible for me not to approve and be made happy for my friend, and my goddaughter's father, that he has this thing to be on fire and sensate about.

It seems, however, almost like a kind of entrapment sometimes, the way he attaches his sympathy to the victims of the fires—the victims, indirectly, of his passion. He thinks he keeps it at arm's length, as do most of the other firemen, but an arm's length is not very far. Some firefighters seem to have no trouble at all shutting out their concerns and sympathies for the lives of the burned. If I am not mistaken (and quite possibly I am), some of them seem sometimes to almost relish the act of putting up that barrier and not letting sympathy invade, diluting the purity of what it is they do and the fervor with which they do it.

But with Kirby it is not that way and in the years I have known him I can see that it has made him more aware of and sympathetic toward structure, and the strength and solace it can give, the support it can have to offer, to people's lives.

So as not to miss any of the calls, I'm hanging out at his house through the Christmas holidays. The baby girl, (Payton, two), is doing all sorts of cute things, and Jean Ann is pregnant with their second child. Kirby gets to keep his other daughter, Kirby Nichole, on Wednesdays as well as alternate weekends, and like any parent he is often aware of the interval of time, sometimes down to the hours, of how long it is before he'll see her.

There are Christmas presents wrapped and set beneath the tree and stockings hanging from the mantel. It doesn't seem that long ago that we were young. Kirby is telling me a little about firefighters' philosophies—not so much about the cross-grid, the latticework, horizontal and vertical, of technical data (the boiling point of ethyl glycol; the incineration point of phosphene gas; the counterclockwise threading of metric and standard lug nuts; the carrying capacities, in units of amperage, voltage, and wattage, of city power lines)—but rather, he's filling me in on the invisible stuff, the important stuff, about how firefighters get along in the world. Not so much about what things are like, inside the burning structures they fight, but instead, more about what things are like inside the men and women who do the fighting.

We're all just sprawled around on the couch, drinking Cokes and eating hamburgers and chips and watching the baby play. We watched a television show (I don't have a TV) that I didn't know existed (ER, about emergency-room stuff—Kirby scoffed at the inanity of the situations, bent and warped and altered from real life to fit some feeble notions of drama) and after that, a movie we'd rented, *Robin Hood*. It was pretty mainstream, pretty stable and secure. It was as mainstream as I'd tasted in a long time. It tasted good.

It was nighttime and we could feel the temperature dropping, could hear the bare branches clacking and waving in the cold front that was moving through the city, riding in like a wave or a gift: a crispness, a coldness, that seemed of course appropriate to Christmas. It would definitely bring fires, and the feeling I got as we sat there watching the movie and waiting for the dispatcher's horn to sound, was that this was not a bad thing. Kirby didn't want anyone's stuff to burn up, nor did he want anyone to get hurt, but I have been around captive falcons right before they go hunting, and bird dogs in the morning before they are turned out into a field, and there was that same calm, steady kind of confidence and anticipation, knowing that the call was going to come, and that he would once again get to test and engage himself against the thing he was, evidently, meant to do.

"Two things," he said, "piss off a firefighter more than anything else. Number one, not having a smoke detector in every room in the house. You don't have to carry out but one burned-up corpse—one charred kid. One's enough. A smoke detector's as simple as it gets. A fire starts, you hear the alarm, and you and your family wake up and walk outside to life. They cost five bucks and if you can't afford 'em the fire department will find a way to get you some.

"Number two gripe is the folks who think a fire's a form of entertainment—as long as it's not their house that burns up." He shook his head. "These silly dumbasses who feel compelled to come get in the way and gawk, or complain, or hell, criticize . . ." So I get to see that part of my fire-altered friend, too. The fires, and the fighting of them, have made him more compassionate to the lives of people in need, but he has been stretched and drawn in the other direction, too, so that he's lost tolerance for stupidity, carelessness, complacency, and I see how important it is to him, this thing he volunteers to do, and how the worst possible thing anyone could ever do would be to accuse a volunteer firefighter—or any other kind, for you do not go into a burning building thinking about your salary, if you have one—of not trying hard enough.

It would be such a mistake on the part of the layperson to underestimate how much they love to fight the fire; it would be a mistake, too, to underestimate the feelings of relief they savor, after they have put the fire down.

We are clean-scrubbed and fresh-dressed from the earlier fire; our smoky, charcoal-smeared clothes are out in the utility room. The washer and dryer are almost always going at his house. I can still smell a little of the smoke on me, but it feels good to be clean. Kirby says that in a long and hot fire the insides of your nostrils will cake black with carbon and that the ebony crust of it, the burned lining, will come tumbling out in fragments for days afterward, and I wonder what the readers of his tax evaluations must think, if they find those black crumbles caught between the pages, like dust from a bag of briquets.

The temperature's dropping fast. We know there's going to be another fire tonight. And about two-thirds of the way through the movie, the call comes.

It's interesting to me the way Kirby and Jean Ann look at each other as they're listening to the dispatcher's description of the fire, and the summons. It's as if, in the listening—independently but together—each is acknowledging the connection they have to each other, and to the fire; as if there are three things in the room, each with a different relationship to the other, and that each time that fire call rings, these connections and obligations— Kirby to Jean Ann, the fire to Kirby, Jean Ann to Kirby—must be acknowledged.

The dispatcher says that it is a structure fire (a building) and that it is "fully involved," which means it is really rocking. Kirby is ready to go but is listening intently; he doesn't want to miss the coordinates. The dispatcher gives the street address. "That's right near my mother's apartments," Jean Ann says. Then the dispatcher gives the name of the apartments, which are her mother's.

"Call her," Kirby says as he and I are leaving. In an instant Jean Ann has, though there is no answer.

It seems to take a long time: a minute to the station, a minute or maybe two or three to get into the station, packed up and suited, and back out. Kirby and I ride in his fire chief's truck with the siren and lights on. This fire is less than half a mile from the one we were just on and it seems to me they want to pop up in certain areas like toadstools after a rain; that there is sometimes perhaps some itch beneath the surface that desires the fires, and it does all it can to summon them, even to the point of encouraging mistakes and clumsiness.

We reach the apartments after four or five minutes of hard driving. We enter the dark complex—we can see smoke and flames—and try to navigate the swirled street patterns, as if in a maze, that will lead us toward that orange glow in the sky. Every left and right turn we take, Kirby says, is taking us toward Jean Ann's mother's apartment—but finally, at the last fork, we see the fire and the other engines and firefighters—we see the burning apartments—and we turn right, where Jean Ann's mother's apartment lies just to the left.

There's nowhere to park without getting in the way of the pumper trucks and their hoses, so Kirby bounces the truck up over the curb and sets it in the grass across the parking lot from the burning buildings, which are an awful sight: tongues of flame racing along the roof eaves, orange fireballs glimpsed through the blackened windows within, and so much thick gray poisonous-looking smoke.

The man who lives in the corner apartment where Kirby has parked his truck on the grass has been watching the scene from behind drawn curtains—all the lights in the complex have been turned off by the firefighters to prevent their being electrocuted as they prepare to enter the flaming structure—and now as we climb out of the big red truck the man who has been peering at the spectacle from behind his curtains comes storming out in a rage, furious that we've encroached upon his territory.

He's a little old man with a chip on his shoulder so large it appears he might have been lying in wait all his life for Kirby to come driving up and park on his lawn, or rather, on the corner of lawn outside the apartment he's renting.

The old man comes hurtling down the slope in his boxer shorts and T-shirt and house slippers, cursing like a banshee—calling out, among other things, "Hey cowboy! Hey cowboy!"—and the old man launches himself at Kirby, becomes airborne, like a flimsy paper kite or some tiny Styrofoam toy glider plane. The old man falls short of his mark however, so that he's rolling around on the ground, still cursing, and now he's on all fours, laboring to get up, so that it looks (and sounds, strangely enough, given the fervor of his exclamations) as if he's praying to Kirby.

Kirby's all adrenalined up—I can tell he's seen a lot, but doesn't know quite how to take this. He stares at the old geezer (who is now upright and kicking with vigor the tires of Kirby's truck with his house shoes), and then Kirby shakes his head to refocus and turns and disappears into the center of the fire to find an assignment, something he can do before his men get here. He hands me a walkie-talkie so I'll look official and tells me to patrol the perimeter and try to keep spectators—of which there are dozens—as far back as possible.

Despite the flames, it's dark, and now in their tinted fire-hat face shields and heavy turnout gear, the firefighters all look the same. There is a tremendous force of energy encircling the fire, the hopeful presence of frantic, industrial might: portable, powerful generators humming on all the trucks, and radios squelching and squalling, and different teams of firefighters running in ordered directions to various sections of the burning complex, their boots heavy on the pavement and across the sodden lawn as ribbons of water surge from taut hoses and cascade onto the flames, slowing the flames' spread but not yet shutting them down.

Walking in circles around the burning apartment, as I'm doing, trying not to hyperventilate at the spectacle, the most dominant impression beyond the speed and power with which things are happening is that this is not some drama staged for the screen on Hollywood but is that seemingly rarest of things, the real thing— and you can see what a living thing, what an awful animal, the fire is. You can see it bulging and writhing; you can tell how, when they apply water to one end, the fire hunkers down in that spot but almost simultaneously billows larger somewhere else.

It's so big. The men and women running into and around it are so tiny.

The suit's heavy as lead. I'm tired just from my frantic circling. When I tell spectators to "get back, please," they ignore me, as if my words of politeness were some insignificant breeze, so that on the next lap I have to shout at them, "Get the fuck back, motherfuckers"—trying to break the spell of hypnosis that is being cast upon them (they are edging ever closer to the fire, drawn, faces upturned) and to replace it, jolt it, with fear.

Some of the firefighters are entering the burning rooms, attacking the fire directly, while others are being deployed into those apartments that are filled with smoke but not yet burning, and are searching those rooms for the young and the elderly, or anyone who might have been felled by the smoke, which is usually what kills the victims, rather than flames or heat. You always check the closets, and under the bed; a lot of times, kids will hide in those places when they're scared, just waiting for the trouble to pass. And they're sure not going to come out and say "Hello, here I am," when some big-booted stranger in a dark mask and scuba gear comes stomping through their house, appearing from out of the smoke swinging a pike staff.

In Larry Brown's wonderful memoir of his firefighting days, *On Fire*, he tells how dogs and cats trapped in a burning house will go get in the bathtub, whether there's any water or not, and how that's always where you find them, dead and curled up, suffocated. Kirby has told me a somewhat similar thing: that if you're trapped in a room that's on fire, or full of smoke, you can open the cabinet under the sink in the bathroom, twist off the U-pipe beneath, and breathe that air, a few minutes' worth of cool air coming from the place wherever it is that the water goes.

It's one thing to read about it in textbooks or to have Kirby tell me about it, in a slow and leisurely storytelling way, over a beer or something, and quite another to see it unfolding in fast motion. I keep circling the burning apartments. Now firefighters are up on the roof, cutting vents into the roof with the machine-roars of their Sawzalls—a type of mega–chain saw—to ventilate the fire, to release heat, to help kill it (when it tries to come rushing through those new vents they will be there waiting for it and will attack it). Other firefighters are still storming into the burning building and smashing at it with their fire tools, evil-looking mauls and pikes. Occasionally I get probing, suspicious looks again from some of the officers with radios, and from the firefighters themselves, but they seem able to sense, in that zone or loop of unspoken communication, that whatever I am doing, though not readily explicable to them, is all right, and not a menace but a help.

I cannot impress, in these sentences, the speed with which things are happening—the speed and force with which problems are evaluated and decisions made.

I see Kirby disappear into the back side of the building, manning, with one other partner, a heavy hose. If you don't have enough people on a hose that's too big, it'll lift you off the ground when the water surges through it, like the trunk of an elephant, and smash you against the roof, then thrash wildly, anaconda-like, deadly brass nozzle flopping and snapping every which way.

Kirby says that when you get into a blackened, still-burning building—unable to see, because of the smoke (flashlights only make it worse)—you always have to go in with a partner. A lot of the time you're crawling around on all fours and you can't even see your partner, even though in those situations you keep in physical contact with him or her—never more than an arm's length away, and if for some reason you do become separated, each partner should freeze and then slowly sweep their fire tool (like an ax) in a circle until they bump it against either their smoke-invisible partner or against their partner's similarly searching ax. Kirby says that's about as scary as it gets: as if you and your partner are crawling to certain death, but that you have to go forward and meet it because it's what you are and what you do, and the fire is what it is, and it's not right for one to exist without or unopposed by the other. Of this, Larry Brown has written, "You have to meet the thing, is what it is . . . and for the firefighter it is the fire. It has to

21

be faced and defeated so that you prove to yourself that you meet the measure of the job. You cannot turn your back on it, as much as you would like to be in cooler air."

You crawl through the fire-gutted, hanging tentacles of electrical wires, Kirby says, knowing the power's been shut off but terrified that some well-meaning onlooker, some dipshit, or even some rookie, is going to notice that the main breaker's been turned off and will flip it back on, thinking it's awful dark, that maybe the firefighters could use a little light.

Kirby says when it gets like that, the senses are incredible—that you feel like you're on another planet—an inflammation of the senses, a hyperawareness, so that you could almost read Braille through the heavy leather gloves: every cell inflamed and fully maxed out with physical and intellectual receptivity. Of course it's addictive—if you survive it.

Kirby says if you get lost in a house where you're fighting a fire, or separated from your partner and can't find your way out, you can drop to your knees and crawl until you come across one of the braided fire hoses. He says there are nubby arrows in the weave of them that always angle back to the source—that by feeling the fabric of the hose you can tell in which direction the pumper truck, and safety, lies, and crawl back out.

If you get trapped by smoke and flame—an injury, perhaps—you can take a knife or an ax and cut a slit in the fire hose. The water will surge straight up through the slit and spread itself in a fan-shaped hissing spray known as a "water curtain," which can keep the fire from sweeping over that area for a few seconds more.

I'm wishing Kirby hadn't gone into the burning building. All I can see is darkness and flames, darkness and flames. It seems like far more firefighters are going in than are coming out. It seems as if the fire is swallowing them. Sometimes during a fire bats will swarm in great flocks, trying to fly back down the chimney, to rescue their young.

I wonder if Jean Ann's ever seen him in a real fire, or only in training fires. (The firefighters relish the destruction of old condemned buildings because often they can obtain permission to torch them—and in so doing, are given the chance to practice, under controlled circumstances, to perfect their craft.)

On their hips, the firefighters each wear PALS, or PASS—Personal Alert Safety Systems. If the firefighter is motionless for thirty seconds, the device emits a piercing shriek, which lets all the other firefighters know one of their members is down—though finding the source of the alarm can be difficult, with all the other noise of the fire and (hopefully) smoke alarms. The wails of the PASS also bounce off ceilings, walls, and floors, further confusing the firefighters. They're taught to freeze in unison when they hear one, control their breathing, open their ear flaps and cup their hands perpendicular to their faces to get as accurate a fix as possible. They're expected, when this happens, to change gears, change mentalities, in a split second—to go from thinking in terms of assault and attack instead to thinking solely of rescue; defense rather than offense.

The PASS can be self-activated, too, by a firefighter in trouble; you don't have to wait the full thirty seconds to deploy it. The trouble is that sometimes firefighters, caught up in the rush of adrenaline upon receiving a fire call, or entering a burning building, get a severe kind of tunnel vision and, despite their training, forget to activate the PASS. And then when they're lying facedown, unconscious from the smoke, it's too fucking late.

It's all darkness and confusion to me, speed and flames. The fire trucks' generators are hooked up to giant fans that are humming and roaring, sawing the night with their sound, and with their cool winds routing the heat and smoke. I hear someone murmur the word *backdraft*, which is the dreaded phenomenon that occurs when a fire, straining against its limits, is compressed by a lack of oxygen, but has nonetheless superheated all the materials around it, almost to the point of spontaneous ignition—a bright chrome teapot leaping suddenly into incandescent flame, or a painting on a wall flashing to fire like a match being struck, or an entire room, or an entire building, and the firefighters within, igniting spontaneously in this manner—and I hear the word again. I can't tell if they mean that one's occurring, or that the fire is approaching the conditions suited for one. (Blackened windows, pressurized gray smoke leaking from beneath doorways and window cracks, windowpanes rattling and trembling their frames.) All that's required for combustion in a situation like this—the whole building superheated to or beyond the ignition point—is the introduction of even a trace more oxygen; the mere opening of a door can give the fire access to the welcoming flood of oxygen.

Now the ranks of the firefighters who are surging around me, running in and out of the building, are carrying the message that one of their number is missing, though they can hear no PASS squall. Immediately I look for Kirby, whom I do not see, but a minute later he appears and begins questioning the squad that's missing one. Kirby wants to know where the firefighter was last seen and what he was last doing, and they point to a second-story bedroom window that is bright with flame and say he was going to try to go in above it, through the attic, and ventilate it.

I can't quite follow what's going on after that, but I hear the term "ventilate" repeated, and rather than bringing a hook-and-ladder truck around, Kirby runs up to the back patio of one of the downstairs apartments; lifts one of those big-ass, black, wrought-iron patio chairs up over his head; runs back out into the yard; takes a couple of frenzied, waltzing spins with it; and hurls it up against the yellow-flame window—and I know that in the morning his forty-year-old back is going to feel that one.

There is another minute or two before word circulates around to us that they found the missing firefighter—that he had gotten dizzy in the heat and smoke up in the attic and had fallen through part of the ceiling and been stuck for a minute or two, but that he pulled himself out and got out all right.

The fight continues.

I continue circling the building, urging people back. It is still drawing onlookers and they're staring, hypnotized—some of them growing more comfortable with it and edging closer. Kirby says he likes to fight a hot fire in cold weather. When it's really cold he relishes going into the burning building, just to warm up.

There are patches of moments where it seems strangely like Mardi Gras: fragments of time and space that rest on the outside of the thing that is going on between the fire and the firefighters, the weave of that thing being cinched tight. On the other side of the parking lot, not thirty yards from the apartment complex that's burning, a forty-ish woman in a loose white terrycloth bathrobe is standing languidly in the darkness of the doorway of her own apartment, watching, smoking a cigarette like a movie star, elbow tucked into one hand, legs crossed, blowing lazy smoke rings as the leaping flames occasionally illuminate her: darkness to light, darkness to light.

Watching Kirby throw that chair through the window reminds me of an image from twenty years ago. There was a pizza restaurant called Major Domo's, just a strip-mall kind of restaurant in Houston, but as a gimmick designed to draw people in, it had a large plate-glass window through which you could watch the chefs, all big swarthy fellows with baker's hats, white aprons, and black handlebar moustaches, as they twirled and tossed immense droopy, saggy flying saucers of dough.

There's no explaining, I think, the surges and hormonal profiles of adolescent blood. For no reason that we knew of then, and still don't, it came into our minds (watching moths flutter against the streetlights, perhaps) to come running up from out of the darkness on summer nights and launch ourselves, hurl ourselves spread-eagled, eyes bulging wide and mouths open in expressions of mock surprise, hurdling through the air (dog-paddling as if in space), and then landing hard against that great vertical pane of glass, striking it so hard as to reverberate it within its frame.

I suppose the object was to try to disrupt the pizza toss—to cause the chefs to pause and stare at us as the pizza, momentarily forgotten, came down on top of them. We never quite got the desired effect, but we did distract them enough to cause a few two-handed saves.

We would hang there against the glass for some fraction of a second as if struck there, like giant tree frogs, before sliding slowly down and then running back off into the night. We struck at random—we might be driving around, bored, and one of us would say, "Let's do a Major Domo tonight"—and the object of the game became, over the course of the summer, to go all the way to the edge, to guess just how hard you could leap against the big plate-glass window without crashing through. We never did, though surely we came close, and it used to please us to no end to consider how it must have affected the lives of the dough tossers: the chefs wondering each morning, perhaps—maybe even upon awakening—whether the window leapers would come that night. And tossing the dough, twirling it, but also, perhaps, nearly always squinting, peering out into the darkness, watching and waiting . . . Sometimes it was more fun to not go by there, and not leap—to let the tension build for days, even weeks.

Another thing the captain of the fire department and I would do, twenty years ago, was pull up at construction sites, after school, and walk right in among the half-framed timbers of a place, with our own hammers and saws, and begin hammering and nailing—pounding goofy little pieces of scrap wood into goofy little places, or fooling with screwdrivers as if checking the preliminary electrical wiring boxes, and calling out instructions and measurements to one another, always appearing brisk and unquestioning, hurling bullshit to the redline, trying to see where it would max out. Subcontractors were forever coming and going, especially on the larger projects, and even now I can remember the deliciousness, the sparkling in the blood as we bluffed our way through work—a thing like adrenaline, but goofier—a yearning for chaos, for making a little disorder out of what we doubtless perceived as too much order, too many constraints and boundaries.

Now he pulls burning people out of buildings, saves their lives and properties—hurls himself against the crumbling, burning city as if single-handedly trying to prop it up. The change amazes both of us. I studied geology in college, learned how time carves valleys and mountains and spreads the plains flat, but time is no slouch either at carving our own lives anew and assembling order of disorder in stretches of time far shorter than the millennia.

★

You can see the fire shrinking as the fighters begin to gain the upper hand. They will always gain the upper hand—no fire lasts forever—and it's only a question of course how much damage will be done before the fire ends. This fire, the apartment fire, is disappearing, and as it does, the apartments seem to be losing what made them alive—flaming, raging, reckless—and are becoming instead the blackened, gutted husk of a thing. Finally, they are only a smoking, sodden ruins, and now there comes the monotony of salvage and clean-up. The firefighters cover everything they can with plastic tarps before moving through the interior, hosing down anything still smoking. This is good firefighting—there's no sense packing up and getting back to the station, tired and dirty, only to have to turn right around and race back out half an hour later because a stray coal or ember found a little breeze and fanned back into flame. It's good public relations work, too, which is always important. Kirby says little things like that—trying to stack the burned furniture out of the way, or protecting what can be protected, in the midst of such carnage, order amid disorder—really helps soften the blow for property owners. You'd be surprised, he says, how much difference it makes to them when they come back to view the damage to notice that someone was thinking about them.

I'm helping carry boxes out from the inside of the hollowed, char-blackened apartment. (Investigations will later show that an untended candle started this fire.) The renters are there and one of the shoeboxes of photos, with which they fled, has spilled its photos, and in the darkness they can't find them. We search with flashlights in the bushes below the second-story window and find them, drenching wet, but still with the likenesses, the images; we salvage them.

Now it is over and the trucks are loading up and pulling away, letting the night fill back in with darkness and silence. The firefighters have shed their coats and glisten with sweat, ghostly like angels in their white T-shirts beneath the suspenders of their fire pants. Char-faced, they guzzle Gatorade and various sugar drinks. They drain their hoses and roll them back up in neat but basic folds; at the station the next day, they will clean them and dry them and refold them into more intricate packages designed for ease and speed of unfolding. They will coil them up in reverse horseshoe folds, straight-finish and Dutchman folds; in flat loads and reverse and split lays, in accordion load folds, and in donut-roll and Twin donut-roll folds. They will practice knots, refill their scuba tanks, clean the trucks until they gleam again, bright as the fire itself. Once a week they will go to a continuing-education class designed to further cram their brains with knowledge that will help them prove counterweights to the fire, and once a month they will go to an all-day training station to stay sharp, whether they have been experiencing any recent fire calls or not; though in a big city like Houston, there will always be fires—some place in it will almost always be burning, and if it is within their territory, they will be rushing to it and grappling with it, as if trying to wrestle it, to press it back into the earth or wherever it came from.

I noticed at these, and other fires I attended, as well as at the training sessions, two basic profiles of individuals. No one person of course will fit any other's profile, but I was struck by how it seemed to me there were only two types of firefighters. (Perhaps if you draw the parameters loose and wide enough, there are only two types of anything.) There seemed to be the thinkers, like Kirby, who loaded their minds with the vertical and horizontal components of possibility—the ones who are able, through repetition and practice, to throw back the awful and intoxicating tunnel vision that can occur in a fire and who instead look down upon the scene (even when involved in the midst of it), as a hawk might look down on a field from two miles up or higher. These men and women are generally the leaders—the captains, the chiefs.

There is also, to complement these, a profile of what could be called, unfairly in many instances, good old boys and girls—men and women who would work just as hard or harder to save your life and property but who prefer to hurl themselves physically at the fire, under orders and command.

It's possible you could call them thrill seekers; they often moonlight as policemen, security guards, and ambulance drivers. And I think the common denominator these hurlers-of-physical-selves have with the thinkers is that they desire, have a need bordering almost on addiction, to feel life deeply, sharply—with either their minds or their bodies—and that they also want to do good, for any of a million different reasons.

This specific, unspoken desire in the blood bonds them as close as family; in many ways it reminds me of the unspokenness of animal language. The sudden leap, without transition, from full stop to full start—usually in the middle of the night—when the dispatcher's horn sounds in each of their homes . . . Kirby's told me that many times he and Jean Ann have been sitting on the couch and have paused and looked at each other just moments before their horn goes off, somehow knowing that a fire is burning in their territory, and that a call is coming through.

A leader like Kirby needs hawk vision—needs the ability to juggle the horizontal and vertical matrices—but he also needs the animal knowledge of the body, the awareness of grace, or its dangerous, confusing absence.

Kirby tells me of one of the first fully involved structure fires for which he was a captain. It was in the home of a trophy big-game hunter. The house was full of smoke and visibility was almost nil, save for the flaming heads of rhinos, lions, elephants, and kudu. They were fighting the fire hard but were losing ground and at great risk of losing contact with each other. The whole time, Kirby was antsy as hell, for this and other inexplicable reasons, and finally he made the decision to withdraw, to get the hell out. They'd done all they could—they'd been called too late—and it was out of hand.

Thirty seconds after he had all the men out, the second floor gave way. It wasn't a typical wood-frame floor, but poured concrete. It smashed pancake-flat onto the space where his firefighters had been crawling only seconds before.

Then, as if for punctuation, the fire found the ammo cache, and the fusillade of large-caliber bullets in vast quantities—ordinance—began.

The firefighters turned their attention to the other surrounding homes; began spraying them down to keep them cool, to keep them from igniting simply from the radiant heat of the house fire next to them. To someone unfamiliar with firefighting, it must have looked like they'd lost their minds—the house in the center burning more or less merrily while the firefighters hosed the hell out of the unburned ones next to it.

Not that he was always cool or graceful, or that he always possessed the hawk vision. Kirby says that on the first structure fire he ever went out on—a green-ass rookie—he got the tunnel vision so badly that he jumped off the truck (his was the first on the scene) and did indeed run into the wrong house, busting the door down to do so, much to the dismay of the occupants inside. They kept asking him why he was in their house and he told them to never mind that, to help him haul the heavy hose up the stairs to the attic, where he believed the fire was hiding.

It seems like a long time ago, that. He's taken to the profession—his other, alternate, second profession—as if he'd been born for it, fitting comfortably into the huge responsibility of captain, and being named Firefighter of the Year by his district.

We're driving home so he can tell Jean Ann it wasn't her mother's apartment that burned, but the one next to it, and that everyone's all right—driving sweat-stained and grubby with the windows down, the cold December air cooling us as if we still carry the heat of the fire with us—and I think about the notion that, all along, Kirby has been ready for this, has been made for this, and has just in the last several years stepped into the fit of it.

We pull up in Kirby's drive. He has saved a baby before, has seen dead people before, has seen people burned up and perforated and lanced and crushed. He has burned himself badly—his body is mottled with ember scars, like constellations—and has torn a knee, twisted an ankle, broken a shoulder, et cetera, et cetera. So far he's always come back from a fire—so far, he always has.

I can feel the relaxation. I can feel the charged new ends of things, the senses whittled sharper. It's very relaxing, very nice.

It's 3:00 a.m. The lights at his house are the only ones lit on the street. Lit up like that, his house looks like a castle.

Jean Ann meets him at the door, as she has hundreds of times, and he meets her.

It's not about being a hero. It's about being alive. It's about being the counterweight to a thing, about being connected to some force that's out there.

We shower, then sleep lightly, waiting for more. He's different from how he was in high school. The fire has altered him.

THE SHINING MARSH

I FEEL LIKE A COUNTRY RUBE as Todd Merendino, a Texas Parks and Wildlife Department biologist, trailers us out into the middle of what looks like a cow pasture. Indeed, there are cow pies sprinkling the pasture, and the perpetrators themselves come shuffling toward us after we have shoved the flat-bottomed boat off its trailer. The cattle edge in even closer, surrounding us, and I'm thinking, *Man, that water, that shining marsh, sure looks a long way off; it's going to be a tough slog to push this heavy thing all the way from here to there.*

But Todd gestures to me to climb up into his strange carriage, and he starts the incredibly loud motor, and suddenly the breeze is in our face and then the early-April brown prairie, with its first few tiny flecks of blue-eyed grass, is hurtling beneath us in a dizzying mosaic, like the old film clips of the pages of a calendar shuttling by with uncontrollable speed.

I knew such things existed, and I knew vaguely what their purpose was and how they functioned—to skim across the top of water so ludicrously shallow it would appear you could just as easily navigate it in your boots and never take on water above those boot tops—but I had no idea they could go across dry land as well.

Here at sea's edge, ibises come as if drawn by a magnet or directed by some divine force.

The tiny castles of crawfish stipple the landscape, and it's like some kind of *Star Wars* phenomenon, as if we're weaving our way through civilizations and palaces. Then, suddenly, we're into the clear, living water of the marsh—two inches of fresh water, maybe three or four. It's more like some kind of fairy tale as we hurtle through and between and amid what I think of as the three elements of time—earth, sky, water—and as a dyed-in-the-wool tree hugger, the fact that it is the fuel of the fourth element, *fire*, in the form of recently ignited fossil hydrocarbons, which is propelling us on this privileged, astonishing voyage, makes me blanch a little.

Just this once, I tell myself, *just one more time.* I'm back in Texas, at the Peach Point Wildlife Management Area, only an hour and a half south and east from where I grew up in Houston, back in the state where as a geologist I learned how to probe the ancient earth below, searching for the very products—oil and gas—that have allowed us to be on this merry journey. In our species' curious, endearing, and maddening way, I find myself trying to rationalize this discrepancy, this problem, to resolve the paradox, to search almost wildly for a way to make amends; to mitigate, seeking balance in an imbalanced world.

We have not yet traveled very far at all, skittering across the shining, shallow water, before there rises suddenly before us a howl of birds—magnificent black-and-white birds with long legs, long bills, long wings—the sky before us filling with them, ibises, so many that it seems we have blundered into the place where all of the world's ibises are congregating, this blue-sky, early-spring day, or perhaps even into the place where ibises come from—erupting as if from some volcanic neck, an outpouring of ibises, a Spindletop of ibises.

Todd cuts the engine and we drift, watching the wave of them above: white-faced ibises, which are not white at all but dark, blackish-appearing in profile, but then iridescent in movement, and white ibises, which are the color of clean snow. Together, the two species roll across the sky like the notes of visible but inaudible music. And once they're a little farther away from us, they quickly settle down and begin feeding once more, striding purposefully through that clear, shallow water with glittering splashes spraying diamond-like around their legs as the wind gusts past them in sheets. They stir and probe the mud, dowser-like, with their incredible bills, plowing and furrowing this vast and near-final flooded prairie of rot and ultimate organicity. A long time ago—three thousand years?—this was an inland bay, but centuries and then millennia of deposition from the great Brazos River have changed all that.

This is the place now where the rich, fine-grained, organic sediments finally settled out, filtered by landscape: the confluence of the San Bernard and Brazos Rivers, the latter one of the most amazing transporters of sediment in this country—in the company of the Mississippi and the Amazon, in that regard—headwatering up in the Panhandle and then winding and curving its way through Texas, until the river finally lies down to rest here on this phenomenally planar delta, bestowing its final gift.

And to that final gift, here at sea's edge, the ibises come as if directed by some divine force. And from the richness of all that sediment, as well as the high-tide yields of the ocean—bounty coming from the north as well as the south—the magnificent beauty of the ibises is born, each bird as fantastic and phenomenal as a lotus from the mire.

Even a non-birder such as myself knows enough, in that first instant of ibis sighting, to gape in slack-jawed, awe-bound reverence—the word *transfixed* comes to mind—and it does not surprise me to discover later, in reading up on these amazing birds, that they've been revered by human cultures for centuries. In *The Birds of Texas*, John L. Tveten writes of the family *Threskiornithidae*, "The sacred ibis was deified as the god Toth by the ancient Egyptians, and the very rare Japanese ibis was declared a national treasure by that government. Ibises have been popular subjects of Japanese and Chinese artists through the ages." And then, with a familiar blush of shame, I read on: "In the United States, on the other hand, hundreds of thousands of white ibises and roseate spoonbills were slaughtered in the late nineteenth century because the feathers were prized for ladies' hats."

Well. Here they are, so many that if Todd, ballast to my ignorance, were to tell me that it is in this last 15,500-acre garden that every last ibis in the world is holed up, stirring the rich muck of delta soup, this writhing rich broth, in search of crabs, snails, crayfish, insects, and all the other proteins it can excavate with its long bill—each bird searching for its own desired, not-yet-fossil fuel, probing and drilling—then I would believe him; that it is behind this one last magic curtain, on this one last special marsh, where all remaining ibises gather in graceful, ancient ceremony.

We stop out on the flats and stare at them through binoculars. The bright light is distorted into shimmering vertical waves similar to the wind-whipped, horizontal water-waves through which the ibises are wading, further accentuating the impression that we have stepped behind a curtain, and into another, older world. How long has it taken to make an ibis, I wonder—ten million years? A hundred million? Rarely have I ever seen one species so wedded to its landscape, so fitted, the sculpted relationship between landscape and species so easily witnessed. It's like looking out at a field of ten thousand grizzly bears, or ten thousand buffalo. It is profound, and we sit there, lulled by the slap of shallow waves against the hull of the boat.

The Freeport Christmas Bird Count, started near here many years ago by birdwatching legend Victor Emanuel when he was a teenager, for a long time held the national record for most sightings in a day—more than three hundred species, all due to the confluence of the two essential habitats: marine and riparian.

How close it all came to the void, however. This area was one of the initial Spanish land grants deeded to Stephen F. Austin's "Old Three Hundred" back in 1821. Austin knew a good thing, and he deeded himself land between Jones Creek and the Brazos in 1830; a portion of Peach Point lies within those old boundaries.

It's big country, but because it's so flat, we can see to the horizon in any direction, and back toward the mainland, the shimmering white shapes of refineries and massive storage tanks blur and waver, magnified by that shimmering light, marking the management area's boundaries. Phillips Petroleum and Dow Chemical once owned thousands of acres in these parts (and still do), but due to various industrial activities elsewhere, the corporations needed to come up with some mitigation to proceed—blood money, we environmentalists call it—and so this amazing spot was protected, though not without a near miss, like a tiny chip in the teeth of fate's gearings.

For a while, during the oil boom of the early 1980s, the Seadock Corporation was planning to turn this area from an inland marsh into a port with an offshore terminal for the world's supertankers. The boom ended though, or else they'd probably still be digging and dredging here, hauling the marsh away, just like that fellow over in Iraq did to his country's native wetlands. The Texas Nature Conservancy bought the property and then sold it to Texas Parks and Wildlife Department (TPWD) in 1987. The refuge now exists as a "sister refuge" with another protected area up in Alberta, in prairie pothole country, and thinking of my own fragmented, vital valley in northwest Montana, the Yaak, I'm envious of Alberta's good fortune. There's so little left to save, really, and our appetites are so immense.

Do the ibises know this? I hope not. Driven by their own fierce hungers, they come to this perfect place, as intent, perhaps, on the universe of crustaceans just a few inches beneath them—the milieu of the sacred past—as they are upon the world above, the world through which they stride. They come soaring in, highly social, in flocks of a hundred, two hundred, gliding on bent wings with their bills angled like dippers, identifying them to us from a great distance, and identifying their needs clearly, unambiguously—to probe and stir, to drill. They fly right over the tops of the sprawling refinery complexes, the seemingly endless phalanx of smokestack and giant storage tanks, as if flying into the heart of the beast itself; nothing can turn back their desire, their need.

Tveten writes: "They move in unison, as if following a choreographed routine, beaks probing the mud ahead. Stride, probe, stride, probe. Occasionally an ibis raises its head to swallow a tasty morsel, then, as if afraid of losing ground, hurries to regain its place in the advancing line. It is one of nature's great ballets."

It is like a ballet, and like a march, too—an army. During the mating season, as their bare facial skin and legs convert springtime's hormones to turn bright scarlet and shiny—as bright as if painted with fingernail polish—they consume even more shellfish, seeking ever more protein for the rigors of the breeding cycle.

The destruction and fragmentation of wetlands is a huge continuing pressure against their survival, as is our heavy use of pesticides and herbicides, particularly in the rice fields. The democratic Brazos does not differentiate between good and bad, but brings all the water it can south and deposits it here, poison and bounty alike. Tveten reports that analyses of the nest failures of ibises along the Texas Coast have revealed "lethal concentrations of dieldrin and other persistent insecticides in the bodies of the nestlings."

We scoot on, pushing up more birds from behind the veil—calories, units of heat, energy expended with each flock's fluttering wave, then energy gained from a new feeding ground. It's all an equation, a swirl, and the slow sultry death of the Brazos feeds and feeds and feeds these amazing birds, as does the ocean, and its tides.

Of the white-faced ibises, Tveten reports: "At close range and in good light, they are unexpectedly beautiful birds," with "the rainbow iridescence of bronze and green and violet" that seems to shimmer across them as they pass through different angles of sunlight. And sometimes, in the flocks that leap up before us and veer away, there are other vast congregations: a battalion of night herons, from behind one curtain of reeds, and in another open stretch, a great assemblage of willets is mixed in with the ubiquitous ibises, each willet less than half the size of the ibises that tower around them, and yet they are all feeding together.

We can never pick it all apart, can never know all of the *whys*—though even if we could, we would then surely be unable to know all of the *whys* of the *whys*—and amid such bounty, it is clear that the mysteries of life extend all the way down, like rich layers of sediment, traveling all the way to the world's core. Such realization, while bathed in such beauty and bounty, produces in us not just awe, but a kind of wonderment, almost like shock—almost like the shock of being loved, and deeply.

Back and forth we skitter, to the perimeters and then to the center, finding birds everywhere. Of course the world needs its many vital, scattered places, each to accept the dispersal of this bounty, but how fiercely it also needs its core places, these late-winter staging grounds that can provide such a rich and continuous feast for all who gather. All are invited; none are turned away. In nature's democracy, the journey north to their various breeding grounds will begin to select them, choosing winners and losers, as well as the lucky ones, and sharpening or breaking each to this strange and shifting world. But here and now, at Peach Point, there is only feasting, only bounty.

We motor on, wind-buffeted in our roaring chariot, across the shining, glittering marsh. We can see distant little mottes of oaks, smudges of forest-green painted in etchings between the blue sky and the winter-browned marsh. Todd refers to these groves or islands of oaks as "migrant traps," which draw the eye of the tiny little songbirds, the azure and vermilion and emerald and lemon and lazuli and crimson travelers, the flecks of eye candy that stun us with their beauty. Such tiny travelers drop down into these increasingly rare forests to take a break from their migration, to rest and feed on the insects found there, and to take refuge against inclement weather. Earlier this morning I had stopped and looked around in a stand of live oaks but had seen nothing, and had presumed that the little migrants were still a bit farther south, unwilling to push on just yet into the teeth of the cold north wind that had swept and scrubbed these blue skies so clean.

Perhaps they are only a day, or even half a day, farther south, hunkered down beneath the canopies of coastal thickets, waiting and listening impatiently; the wind is supposed to die down by evening. Perhaps as soon as I leave Peach Point this afternoon, they will come surging north—strategic, determined, relentless. Surely they are still out there, bright in the world. We know their numbers, as well as their habitats, are dwindling, but surely this is not the year, yet, when they no longer come.

Nor are we disappointed by this day's or two days' delay. What we are seeing already is more than enough, is like some spectacle from Africa, or the Everglades or Saskatchewan.

Again, I feel a blush of shame, to be perched out here on the bow of a boat this lovely cold day, while others of my kind are out in the sands of the Middle East, lost and burning; shooting and bombing and killing and being killed.

What a wake-up call, what a moral challenge, for environmentalists. What a crucible for our bedrock faith that the natural world still matters, has always mattered, through thick and thin; that as long as there are still patches or gardens of beauty in the world, uncompromised and existing for a purpose beyond our own immediate needs or desires, then almost any kind of redemption or recovery can be dreamed and imagined, even accomplished.

This is what it looked like before we began to make mistakes. This is what it looked like before things started to go bad.

This is how our hearts used to feel, as children.

When I was a geologist—a fifth of a century ago—I used to explore long-buried landscapes not all that distant from this one, in north Mississippi, probing and pecking little eight-and-five-eighths-inch holes into Paleozoic deltas and offshore bars. With my pencil and eraser, I used to wander across old bays and estuaries, wading through the wave-tossed detritus of dissolved mountains, looking for buried treasure—what we called "production," a euphemism little different from that of either a farmer or a biologist—and when we succeeded in discovering what we were looking for, we would turn our maps over to our engineers, who would perform all sorts of complicated equations designed to tell us how many acre-feet of oil we had discovered.

Looking out at this vast sheet of shining water, I'm reminded again of that phrase, acre-feet, for although the volume of this marsh might not possess as much water as even a medium-sized reservoir of oil, it is the distribution and reliability that matters most of all—the fact that it is even here at all—and that it has come so far to get here, and that the open space is here to receive and hold that water, as well as all those tons, all those acre-feet, of sediment, shellfish, and history.

It has been a long time since I have felt in Texas that in ecological terms we are rich with anything. But here, perched atop a civilization far more ancient than that of Babylon, in this little 15,500-acre garden—a sanctuary, a little park—I feel that way once more, feel it again even more wondrously than I did in childhood, before I became aware of the diminishment of things and the erosion of boundaries.

And forgive my gluttony, but I want more. Like some crazed imperialist, even in the midst of such concentrated, focused bounty, I find myself wondering, Where will they all go from here, and will the way be safe for them? And I want more for them.

We move oceanward, out into more shining space, and I'm

forced again to consider the hairbreadth changes, the near misses that lead to the Big Events that change history. If the oil boom of the early eighties had crested a few months earlier—not eons or millennia, but months—we might be motoring across sixty feet of water instead of six inches. There might be only a few laughing gulls circling overhead, or maybe nothing at all. Perhaps we would be surrounded by looming tankers, shining in the sun, their decks towering sixty feet above us.

Instead, we come into a shallow saltwater bay where crab traps bob in gunmetal-gray waves and where the calceus of oyster shells are exposed to the wind-whipped low tides of late winter. We pause near a sandbar and study a congregation of willets, gulls and black-necked stilts, each bird distinct, the gulls hopping up into the wind and catching air and then flaring, and the stilts accelerating their soldierly march somewhat, but still hunting and searching, striding as if in synchrony to the beat of some inaudible rap music, and the brown little willets, with their shorter legs, seeming more furtive, even anxious.

Various flocks settle down, too, after their initial skittishness, and return to the exact place they were feeding and gathering before our approach: as if there exists, after all, a plan, a pattern, and although we tend to see the world as random, it is all woven together like one of those maddening five-thousand-piece puzzles that sits assembled in some lakeside summer cottage, pieced together during a week of rainy weather by unknown visitors maybe fifty years ago; and that despite the momentary disruption caused by our sudden and noisome arrival, all the puzzle pieces must, sooner or later, settle back down into their slots and niches and crevices.

This is a dangerous conceit, and yet out here in the middle of Peach Point, that is how it appears, this one day. And if on this one day, then why not also on all others, now and forever more, no matter what?

Perhaps if this spit was here fifty and sixty years ago, red wolves might have stood on its shores, waiting for bounty to come rolling in. Perhaps, fifty and sixty years from now, whooping cranes will stand in this mud once again, leaving splayed tracks as large as a man's hand.

Does it seem there are fewer and fewer nations of the living, and more and more nations of the gone-away, laid down in the layers of the past like fine-grained Brazos sediment? Does it seem sometimes that the unraveling might not just stop or cease with the unbraiding of cranes and songbirds, wetlands, marshes, and red wolves, but instead might keep on going, falling apart twist by twist?

And if it does, what force—what loving force—cares or desires to reassemble those braids, and in what manner?

I ask Todd what the most challenging part of his job is. I expect him to say it's managing water flows in an era of diminished availability of that most vital of resources. I try to imagine what a gauntlet it is for a gallon of water that begins somewhere up in North Texas, in the Brazos headwaters, or around Glen Rose, up behind the dam at Possum Kingdom Lake—how difficult it is for that gallon to make it all the way to the coast, and in so doing, carry with it the nutrients that are as critical to this ecosystem as is the dissolved oxygen in your or my red blood.

I would have thought that would be the hardest part: juggling the water, shuttling the puzzle pieces of habitat need and water levels for each individual species each season, like some biological bed-and-breakfast host trying to remember the precise and various needs of an ever-changing assemblage of rushing-through guests.

But Todd tells me that's the easy part—that as far as the water goes, "Either you have it or you don't." If it's not there in certain years, there's nothing you can do but just wait.

The prescribed burns, designed to improve prairie habitat, are hard to coordinate, he says, because they make so much smoke for "the city," by which I presume he means Houston, just to the north (which in 2000 bypassed Los Angeles as possessor of the most polluted air in the nation)—and the mosquitoes can make his job pretty rough, too. "You can't imagine," he says, "it's unbearable"—and yet, he bears it—and when I ask him what his favorite time of year is, he says it's right now, mid-February through mid-April, during the peak of bird activity, before the mosquitoes get bad, and before the heat returns.

The hardest thing, he says, is the vegetative manipulation: trying to keep out the encroachment of woody debris, trying to knock back the invasive, nonnative species such as Chinese tallow, while promoting the recovery of the natives that are so wedded to this marsh: bushy bluegrass, eastern Baccharis, seashore Paspalum, jointed flatsedge (which the ever-expanding numbers of snow geese devastate).

Back at the shop, Todd shows me around his office, talks a little more about the mechanics of airboats, including some horror stories about getting stranded far out in the marsh. He tells me about the bacopa, a creeping vine that the airboat can skitter over when it's wet, but when it's dried out, it becomes a gripping net of splayed fingers that snares the boat and will not allow passage. And then it's time to leave, and for Todd to get back to the little remnant of his weekend. We say our good-byes—and because I still have a few hours left to kill, I take some old back roads, or what I remember from thirty years ago as being back roads.

And for a little while—in the first faint buffer beyond the refuge—things are somewhat as I remember them. I stop outside one large cotton field and park beneath a giant oak and lean my seat back and nap for a while, sleeping the deep sleep of one whose senses have been overstimulated, and for whom catatonia is now almost an antidote, recompense for the rigors of having been so charged earlier. For a little while I dream that the ibises are still soaring above me in waves, but then I sink even deeper and just sleep.

When I awaken, about an hour later, the north wind has stilled, and the ibises are still dancing in my head.

Sometimes I think that scientists like Todd might come as close to fulfilling the role of distant observer as anyone here among the living is able. They can look at a delta landscape and rather than fretting about why the wingtips of snow geese are black, can instead evaluate this entire buried, once-upon-a-time bay in terms of tons-of-protein-per-acre: as if all of life in this one landscape is but an evolving recipe, a great cauldron slowly simmering through the seasons; as if over the course of only a single day, there is a great stewing broth of shellfish, sunlight, vegetation, feldspar, potassium.

Whose recipe, then? Who dreamed, and continues to dream, the things that have arisen from this broth? How many infinite ways are there to distribute, then redistribute, these rations, these elements, these nutrients? Pause in the stirring at any one point in the recipe and an entire other story or species might leap up from the creation; toss in another pinch, and something else? No one will ever know or understand or even dream it all; in the end, we can only witness.

What does it take to support an ibis—or ten thousand ibises— when those same tons-per-acre could support instead another story, an equal biomass of sparrows and starlings?

All life is spectacular, and in its brief flash, sacred. But all things being equal, I will choose ibises.

MOON STORY

THIS IS NOT AN ECLIPSE STORY.

I grew up in Houston in the 1950s, 1960s and early 1970s, so yeah, the moon shot was a pretty big deal. One of the Apollo astronauts was from nearby LaGrange, where my mother grew up—not a moonwalker, but one of the first ones to get blasted away from this sweet blue planet, out into the unknown darkness, to the moon and around and then back, and returning to tell about it.

My own orbit from those days is widening, casting further and farther toward what someday I suppose will be the territory of old age—outer darkness, with only the cold pinpricks of stars for company, while far below and closer to the warm center run and laugh and play the living, almost scurrying, though also with a leisure that approaches nonchalance, even as intergalactic static crackles and bounces off the dry skin of an old outlander like pellets of stinging hail dimpling the fragile heat shield of a spacecraft . . . Look how *small* they are all becoming below, the young, as one's orbit widens, with the distance between one year and the next becoming smaller, like the growth rings of an old tree bunching up out at the perimeter, too close together now to even count.

From those childhood days, I remember the cool NASA baseball caps. I had one as recently as last year, with its whirling proton loop, atomic-orbit emblem—until my pup, a French Brittany with the decidedly un-French name, Otis—chewed it to blue-and-white shards. (From what oil well first came the plastic that made the hatband? I mean, what farmer's field? What year, and where was I, and what was I doing when that black-green oil first rushed up the borehole? And what of the days before any of us existed? What dinosaur lay down his or her sleepy head in the Paleozoic swamp and slept forever, being blanketed then with mud and leaves and the slowly warming rising waters, dissolving to no longer be a dinosaur but instead a soup of carbon and hydrogen, baking and sliding away, up one fault and down another, traveling beneath the surface as it had once in its brief assembly traveled above the surface; ascending, finally, to an anticline with an impermeable cap, like the dome of a cathedral, and pausing there, trapped for eons, and reassembling into oil, before the drill bit—1955? 1958? 1963?—pierced the crypt, released the oil, sent it to the plastics factory, where the hat I wore as a child was birthed?)

Farther. The living are specks. As one ages, time compresses. We perceived, believed, fairly early—in our mid-twenties or thirties—that time is circular, like the four seasons, or what used to be the four seasons, before we drilled too many holes in the earth. (It is not the moon that is made of Swiss cheese, but our own sweet earth. There are experimental technologies that can convert carbon dioxide into a chalky solid, and it's theorized we could use this solid—in paste form—to fill in every well we ever drilled, burying the carbon we burned and used, for a while.)

My own belief is that the genie is out of the bottle; it's hard even in the fiction of science fiction to imagine filling not just every old borehole, sucking CO_2 out of the sky and putting it back in the ground it came from, like putty or cement, repairing or patching a fractured, shifting, quaking substructure with the brittle paste of CO_2 chalk.

And yet I'd like to believe. Where I live now, in northwest Montana, is the site of the world's largest asbestos mine. The ore there contains a certain kind of asbestos, tremolite, the mineralization of which results in its fibers being extraordinarily tiny. Seen under the microscope, they resemble quilled arrows with barbed arrowheads; they lodge in the lungs and stomach lining and then work their way inward, a billion microscopic darts fired by unseen archers. The word *Yaak* is Kootenai for arrow, for the way the Yaak River charges down out of the mountains and into the curved bow of the Kootenai River, largest tributary to the Columbia. There used to be porcupines up here but they have vanished in only the last fifteen to twenty years. My dogs, especially Point, were always getting into them; the barbed quills made it hard to pull them from the dogs, always resulting in much blood and tissue trauma as I wrenched them free. Indigenous folklore refers to porcupines as the Old People of the mountains, and prophesied that when porcupines disappear from a landscape, it means the landscape is in deep illness.

Time may indeed be circular, for the centripetal pull of it out here on the farther perimeters is starting to feel pretty enormous. What if we could suck all the asbestos fibers out of the air around Libby and convert it, like that CO_2, to a solid form, able then to be buried deep? Future generations might know this valley, the Treasure Valley, for its beauty without the bittersweetness of such scourge, such price, awaiting all who breathe.

I meant to be writing about the moon and how I first came to see it, in Texas, but I feel compelled to say a few words about Point. He was the sentinel case of mesothelioma in a pet in Lincoln County. Mesothelioma hits hard and quick; you have six weeks, max. It's best to have one's affairs in order. When it hit him, I drained the pinkish cancer fluid from his stomach with a syringe each night before we went hunting the next day. God, he died hard, swelling like a pumpkin every day, but still tottering on, hunting even on his last day of life, until I realized I was torturing us both, and I had to ket him go, had to release him to that which was pulling at him so hard.

★

In high school, Einstein's elegant $E = mc^2$ was easily memorized, but the assumption of constancy seems an assumption that gets us in trouble in all other matters. Maybe he meant constancy in the moment, the split second in which the equation was applied, but for a long time the string-theory people have been saying nothing we see is a constant, nor can we, nor they, be 100 percent sure is real, instead calling all matter, all *things*, an extreme likelihood of quivering assemblages always in motion, assemblages of smaller things arranged to look like, feel like, the thing we in turn (also a swirling arrangement of matter at any point in time) are feeling, touching, smelling, hearing, tasting, identify as real.

(I often think too that if Einstein had, instead of labeling space as being the thing relative to time, referred to it as place, we all would have done better in school. Place, not space. A positive, tactile thing, mortal. *Place*: the Back 40, the Panhandle, Indian territory, Madagascar, what-have-you, rather than an invisible thing, *space*, as in outer space, and the association of nothingness. A little frozen rock dust, ice crystals at the end of comets. A smear of yellow in all-else blackness.)

As our landscape, our place or space, becomes more fragmented and poisoned, burned, eroded, flooded, and paved, and as our relationship with time also explodes—all of us moving faster and faster, dervishes until we can whirl no more, and as we must lie down upon that broken landscape, the broken space across which our churning altered version of time howls—well, what happens next? Does even our own certainty, or the *likelihood* of us, begin to doubt us, until one by one we each and all begin to vanish, as if to the Rapture?

Or what if we are eradicating—squandering, even—the possibility for and of a rapture, and an afterlife? For if we destroy the land and wound mortally the concept of time-here-below, does not the concept of or likelihood of beyond-time also go down with that sinking ship?

★

"No ideas but in things," wrote William Carlos Williams, less than a generation after Einstein, as if not so much resisting but instead modifying his equation. Williams's dictum resounds more with the Texan in me, and the boy I was at ten who, every time my mother drove me across town to the Houston Museum of Natural History, ran straight to the exhibit of moon rocks. In my memory, I recall there being a small handful on a plain-white surface, nondescript in every way. The geologist I would one day become might describe them as appearing clastic, dry, friable, with an apparent low level of compaction—mafic, brecciated igneous, possibly alkaline? They looked almost chalky, like the pale carbonates and sandstones of the hill country, though even as a child I noted the obvious lack of fossils. But weren't those tiny vesicles testament to gases, suggesting the possibility of a once-upon-a-time oxygen component? And speaking of air—how did the astronauts do *that*? How could they carry that much air with them, or that much water?

What I remember most, beyond the moon rocks' extraordinarily dull dirt color, was my desire to touch them, and my still-dogged if not now–slightly diminished belief that because they were different, rare, hard-gotten, other, they possessed power. They *had* to be treasure.

And if so, why were they displayed so casually—a typed index card stating "Moon Rocks?" There was certainly no need for source or dateline.

Surely they contained such power—radioactive or otherwise— that a mere three-eighths-inch plexiglass could not contain them. I hovered; paced, stalked round and round the small handful of squarish buff-colored stones. Was it a joke? Were the sapphires, moon diamonds, amythest, and beryllium in vaults somewhere else while the astronauts pranked us with these chunks of road rubble they'd picked up on their way home from the airport?

I drifted away. The other things—the living—pulled me. The aquariums, brilliant with tropical fish; the huge-eyed little caiman sunning beneath its heat lamp. No one had a clue then what global warming was. It was upon us but we could not see it. Or we could see it but we did not notice it. The baby snapping turtle, black as tar, as elegant underwater as a ballet dancer, his long Stegosaurus tail trailing, ruddering, as his oversized feet, with claws like a grizzly's, waved in slow motion. His red eyes were studded with an asterisk for each pupil, leading one to suppose he perceived a different world than the one I beheld. And which of us was to argue the other's reality?

The rocks were an embarrassment. The geologist I would become wished the astronauts had stayed longer, dug deeper, searched farther. Climbed a mountain. Gone around to the back side. To have not returned until they found something better.

★

The moon. I believed then and guess I still do that the landing really happened. Though I do sometimes wonder, why has no one gone back?

I know NASA wasn't all about the moon—that one little speck of light out there in so much darkness—but it's interesting to me that I grew up in a culture where often the dominant association with any mention of the moon was to "shoot" it, to launch missiles or rockets at it. At the other end of the spectrum, there was plenty of lame poetry about the moon and stars, dewy meadows, and so forth.

And yet, other times, it could be so great. The moon so abundant, so present in literature.

Walker Percy, from The Moviegoer:

The train has stopped and our car stands high in the air, squarely above a city street. The nearly full moon swims through streaming ragtags of cloud and sheds a brilliant light on the Capitol dome and the spanking new glass-and-steel office buildings and the empty street with its glittering street-car track. Not a soul is in sight. Far away, beyond the wings of the Capitol building stretch the dark tree-covered hills and the twinkling lights of the town. By some trick of moon-light the city seems white as snow and never-tenanted; it sleeps away on its hilltop like the holy city of Zion.

Amy Hempel:

"Tell me things I won't mind forgetting," she said. "Make it useless stuff or skip it."

I began. I told her insects fly through rain, missing every drop, never getting wet. I told her no one in America owned a tape recorder before Bing Crosby did. I told her the shape of the moon is like a banana—you see it looking full, you're seeing it end-on.

The poet Jim Harrison, in "Sketch For A Job-Application Blank":

My left eye is blind and jogs like
a milky sparrow in its socket . . .

. . . I strain for a lunar arrogance. . . .
Light macerates
the lamp infects
warmth, more warmth, I cry).

And, in "Returning At Night":

. . . in the root cellar
the potato sprouts
creeping through the door
glisten white and tubular
in the third phase
of the moon.

Patty Griffin does the best cover of "Moon River." Nanci Griffith's "Once in a Very Blue Moon" is very fine, as is (duh) CCR's "Bad Moon Rising." (I'm told two of the Fogerty brothers lived in the Yaak Valley when they were younger; how I wish to believe that the lyrics to "Run Through the Jungle" were informed by that wild if unprotected landscape.) Oh, yeah—like I'm gonna forget—Neil Young's "Harvest Moon," also covered admirably by The Shook Twins.

It was Emmylou Harris, long ago, whose "Quarter Moon in a Ten Cent Town" first suggested to me that a moon in art need not always be perfectly round to be noticed or appreciated.

★

In high school, after going to an Astros game with my best friend, Kirby, I got lost in the Astrodome parking lot, looking for where we'd parked. This was in the days before beepers. We had to wait for the other fifty thousand people to leave. I can't remember if the moon was out or not. Even then, Houston was a big city; downtown often cast a fizz of light, an inverted umbrella dome of fuzzy gold light.

I went to one of the original Astros' games, a Cub Scout deal where for some reason we went on a school night. It ended up being what for a long time was the longest extra-inning game in major-league history, a 1–0 contest that finally ended in the twenty-fourth inning. I can't remember who won, but the randomness of it remains with me: the first game I ever went to. We left early—fourteenth, fifteenth inning?—and had to read about how it ended in the morning paper, which just barely was able to capture the result before going to press. Who ever dreamed, back then, that newspapers would one day go away? What other fantastic turnings of fate and history remain out ahead of us, unseen, unscented?

★

My dad, a geophysicist and a hunter, and my mother, a schoolteacher before I was born, saw to it that I had a taste for nature, not just in the museums but in the woods. We would go deer hunting every fall up in the hill country, at a place we called the deer pasture. A wild, feral land of incredible stargazing: Gillespie County. One night when my cousin Randy and I were outside gathering firewood, a meteor tore through the curtain of black sky like a rock thrown through the thinnest pane of creek ice. We looked up and saw it go sizzling past, scorching and sparking, then nothing but gray smoke, with the stench of burned stone. Its velocity might have carried it another five or ten miles past us. Still, I look for that stone yearly, and I like to imagine I might yet come across it and will, when I do, somehow recognize it when I see it. That it will be so much more superior to the moon rocks of my youth.

My youngest brother, B. J., and I were dinking around at the deer pasture one summer when I decided to pursue a goal that had long intrigued me: to climb nearby X Mountain, even though it was on someone else's property. In Texas, the feudal notion of private property, the sanctity of personal territory and ownership, is deeply entrenched, ridiculous as it might seem from a biological perspective. The gridwork of fence posts and barbed wire lattices the entire state as if dicing it into so many croutons.

Every strand holds tufts of hair or fur or feathers from all the other passers-through but our own kind.

I had been living in Montana long enough by that point to have become more than comfortable with the concept of the commons.

A little about *X* Mountain; a little about the rumpled hill country, the ragged land updip from the Balcones Escarpment. Geology's cuts and cleavings are almost always beautiful, made slowly more sinuous by time and wandering like a beach's strandline of before and after. We rip with saws, we bulldoze straight lines through the forest, we dig trenches for pipelines; our railroad lines and interstates fire through the forest and across the prairies and even beneath the seas like arrows fired or like missiles disgorged from silos tilted onto their sides so that they now face us and only us directly, rather than pointed with a trajectory toward Siberia, the Irkutsk, Iceland, Moscow. Nature is rarely if ever linear or even geometric . . .

I digress. I've exceeded the orbital pull of the subject. The Texas hill country contains some of the oldest stone in the world that can be found at the surface: pre-Cambrian granite, and Cambrian sandstone, what was once the floor of the new-made world, the dawn of all life, simple one- and then multi-celled organisms spinning in the sunlit seas, being drawn forward and backward with the tide—organisms so tiny they can't even be seen in the stone in which they now exist forever. Though I like to think sometimes that when I'm building a stone wall or a flagstone driveway with those rocks, and I drop one, releasing a wisp of arid dust, what I see and smell in that plume is the ground-up ephemera of what life was like a billion years ago: the first scent of us and our kind approaching that slow long on-ramp.

It is a pleasing smell, and while it arouses no memories in me other than the here and now—hot summer days working in the rock fields with my family, making slow order out of disorder, the disassembled and broken becoming beautiful and whole once more, scent of bluebonnets with solitary bumblebees feasting on their nectar, and grasshoppers rattle-clacking away with wings spread, gliding, the most primitive of flying machines, and yet the most enduring—Ah, shit. Where was I? *Contact.*

The deer pasture where we hunt also possesses some of the world's oldest granite—rock older than even the Cambrian sandstone that crept in sediment by sediment, atop the granite's now-cooled but once-upon-a-time tongues of flame, the mineral-rich magma surging upward along any vertical fissure it could find, any thinness or weakness in the overlying Cambrian strata. And, where it could find no weakness, creating one: the thing which had never seen sunlight before, the minerals that have existed in the great furnaces near earth's dense center, demanding their own time in the sun.

Some made it out and cooled rapidly; others made it almost all the way out, but not quite. Though cooling now, far from the maddening heat and resting just beneath the surface, the minerals in that magma had all the time in the world to rearrange themselves according to their polarities and chemical charges and valences, spinning and rotating as if governed by magnets or twin poles, their earth-center miles below, and the strange moon rock in the sky, which was maybe related to them or maybe not.

It was in this slow, just-beneath-the-surface cooling that great beauty was achieved. The crystals began adhering to one another, blossoming into fantastic spires and cathedrals, with each elemental mineral, and each assemblage of elements, having all the time in the world to form and grow. These are the crystals—the slow crystals—I wanted to believe comprised the heart and soul, the inner being, of the moon. *Dig deeper.*

★

What is the sound of the psychic stall horn, the command to point the nose back down now or be lost forever, when one lives so far from humanity in a place like the Yaak Valley, talking only to one's dogs and even then not much, using hand signals—drifting, keeping the crazed world, the lunatic world, at arm's distance, or beyond arm's distance? It's a hermit existence some of us fit better than others. It's the way some are meant to be. Moonlike, in that regard, I guess you'd have to say. "We loved the earth but could not stay"—Wallace Stevens.

At the deer pasture, B.J. and I prepared to climb over the barbed-wire fence and set out toward the previously mythic X Mountain. Because it was on the other side of fences, it seemed far away. In reality, it was ludicrously close; we were there in a blink.

But before we got there—in that first fence crossing—I snagged my leg on the taut and newly strung barbed wire.

The difference between old rusted barbed wire and the moonbright silver knife blade of the taut unblemished product, so ratcheted to its full tensile stretch that the wind passing over it causes it to hum a faint, keen dog whistle, is like the difference between, I don't know, cooked and uncooked spaghetti.

I stood on the firm lowermost strand and lifted my other foot toward to the top strand, which is what one can do when they're stretched that tight. But even then, there's usually a little stretch or sag beneath one's full weight. I was expecting it, and when there wasn't, I wobbled for a moment, and in so doing I raked my calf across one of the fence's twisted teeth, the tip of a single barb sharper than the point of a knife.

It was the kind of wound that cuts so cleanly there is no pain, only the sudden tickle of blood's wetness now on skin. It was not cool enough for the blood to steam but the blood went from warm to cold quickly as it trickled down my leg and into my sock. In John Prine's great song, "Lake Marie," he pauses to query the listener: "You know what blood looks like in a black-and-white video? *Shadows!* That's what it looks like. *Shadows.*"

I'd never quite understood the leap in allusion there, but looking at my leg in that hyper-brilliant silver-blue light, I was reminded immediately of the song. The blood had the gleaming quality to it of the scorch of old-time flashbulbs. And it was definitely the darkest thing in that mercuric, floodlit world—the only dark thing, I realized, which might have been what Prine was seeing and describing.

The tear—the slice, slash, gash—was in the balled-up meat of the calf muscle. *That one's gonna leave a scar*, I thought—*who needs tattoos?* And as we proceeded on toward the hill, the mythic mesa we had seen all our lives, but, due to the vagaries of private property—land the colonists took from Mexico, who had taken it, if in name only, from the Comanches, who may or may not have taken it from someone before them (the Athabaskans?)—grew smaller the closer we got.

There were shadows now. We passed through a grove of small oaks, the shadows as dark as the trunks of the trees themselves, and I left a smear of blood on blades of grass and on the silver-fire leaves of agarita and shin oak.

We started up the steep slope, but with every step, the mountain before us shrank until it could not even really be called a hill. It was a flat-topped bump, a little neck of caliche, limestone, remnant of older sea-times, compressed to chalk; but not as ancient as what had once sat atop, and with many of its once-upon-a-time contemporary chalk-strata eroded, ghost-whispered tumbling downstream back toward the new ocean, the Gulf.

We stood on it, looked out. I felt like a child. I was, what, maybe forty? Perhaps not even.

The moonlight bathed us as we strolled around the hill's flat top and through its scrubby wind-blasted juniper. I know this is a wretched cliché, moonlight *bathing*, but it's true; it poured down and over us as if molten silver. Sometimes a cliché is a cliché for a reason. It was brighter than most daylight yet there was no danger of moonburn.

The reversal in scale—the grand becoming almost minute—made me dizzy, as did the moonlight itself. Back when photographs were taken with cameras, not phones, and you took the film to a print shop for developing, you had to look at the strip of negatives to decide which reprints you wanted, if any, on those sepia strips. Dark became ghostly bright, and light became unseeable dark; and on the mesa I felt I was getting a glimpse of the way the world really was, if not to me, then to someone—someone else's reality—and whether that was raccoon or scorpion, bumblebee or night-blooming cirrus, hummingbird or swan, I could not say, only that we were in it.

The top of this great mountain—visible from thirty miles away—was not much larger than some of the shoulder-to-shoulder suburban lawns where I had grown up in middle-class Houston. It was about the size of a burger joint's gravel parking lot.

And yet it was so level, in a land where nothing else was. We walked around on top, feeling much closer to the moon now—hundreds of miles closer, rather than a hundred feet. A jackrabbit, pale as bone, looking like a snowshoe hare in winter, or the white rabbit in a magic trick, leapt from hiding and dashed away. And at the southern end of the mesa, just as I was about to turn around and go back to the other end, I noticed something I might not have seen in daylight: smooth, white, round river stones, atypical for that country, spaced evenly in an arc.

They were grown over with grass and lichens, but the moonlight brought them out in bony relief. Now I could see more of them, each no larger than a skull, but enough of them, I realized, to form a circle. The circle was grown over with grass and low juniper. But it was by god a real tepee ring, which made sense to me, though I'd never seen one around here, only in Montana.

What was a hundred and twenty-five years to a stone, or even the placement of a stone?

I didn't really mind being up there, uninvited by the absentee landowner, who simply had his cattle grazing below, but I was a little rattled by having stumbled into a ceremonial spot uninvited. It had long been unused, of course, but still. The incredible light made me feel super-illuminated in a way I did not want to be, and I apologized for barging in, and we made our way back down, with my leg still painting bright red the low vegetation through which we passed. Indian paintbrush, it's called, *Castilleja indivisa*; one of the perhaps hundred thousand or so microaggressions with which we bruise our way through the world daily.

We made our way down the steep slope following a trail worn not by humans but by the hooves of deer—too steep for cattle, which was likely why the ring was still intact—and walked back toward the silver glimmering fence.

We had not gone far at all when we encountered an immense white-tailed buck, his velveted antlers glowing, as if he carried above him a silver nest of fire.

Big bucks like that are always nocturnal. This one however looked uncomfortable, as if he was being called upon to *swim* through that silver light. It was so strange and thick it seemed like a chunk of light, elemental, like a mineral, rather than reflected waves of light.

After watching us for a few seconds, he turned and ran and vaulted high over the fence, arching like a rainbow, with not even the tip of a hoof touching the top strand. He landed lightly and continued on into the thick juniper beyond, bobbing like a spark: the living, taking refuge in the living.

We approached the same illuminated fence, touched it first, as if it might be hot, and then climbed carefully over it; there could be no squeezing through or under it.

The Old Ones who had sat up on that little hill—who were

they, how long had they sat there, what thoughts had they considered? Where were they now, and will each of us one day become just as invisible? It seemed impossible, yet I knew it was so. Still, it seemed to me that if one lived, burned brightly enough, one might exist always as a kind of echo, or a shadow, in the way that, in beholding the mirror of the moon, we are seeing an echo of the sunlight that was cast many years ago—light-years—and which, reflected, falls down upon us, the echo of an echo, encasing us as if in amber.

A suspect theorem, and yet, what is the downside in believing it, or even hoping?

It was hard to imagine, however, that there could be much downside in the just-enduring, in the hanging-on—the attenuation of a once-bright burning by echo or reflection. Come what may when darkness falls, I find I difficult to believe we are not sometimes already in some sort of betranced afterlife, walking around on petrified ocean floors that are a billion years old, following caliche roads white as summer clouds, all of us bathed—sometimes—in silver.

It seems important to live as if this is all there is, and if something remains or carries forward for a while after we dive back down into the soil, then so be it. But now! On a good day—on the best days—who would want anything more?

★

Much is made of the moon's pull on tides, and of the way it scrambles our soft brains, pulls them this way and that. D. H. Lawrence believed such tugging reveals who we really are—the raw soup of us still so newly emerged in the world that, evolutionarily speaking, we are but jellyfish, still being shaped, molded, rolled around; an experiment, a farther braiding off the ancient tree of all-other-life. Not the trunk, by any means.

The same man who wrote, "Blood knowledge. . . . Oh, what

a catastrophe for man when he cut himself off from the rhythm of the year, from his unison with the sun and the earth. What a catastrophe, what a maiming of love when it was made a personal, merely personal feeling, taken away from the rising and setting of the sun, and cut off from the magical connection of the solstice and equinox. This is what is wrong with us. We are bleeding at the roots." He also announced, more famously, "The essential American soul is hard, isolate, stoic, and a killer. It has never yet melted."

Also this: Cormac McCarthy, from his novel, *No Country for Old Men*."It was cold and there was snow on the ground and he rode past me and kept on goin. Never said nothin. He just rode on past and he had his blanket wrapped around him and he had his head down and when he rode past I seen he was carryin fire in a horn the way people used to do and I could see the horn from the light inside of it. About the color of the moon."

As with the previous pondering about the half-life of any echo of our physical selves remaining after we've moved on to (fill in the blank, Elysian fields, greener pastures, better things, just rewards), I don't presume to wax about what comes next—not even tomorrow.

As one of the last or next-to-last generations before the heavily cloned or the lightly modified begin to walk among us, it can often seem as much like game-over for Homo sapiens as it must have, at some point, for Neanderthals, or Cro-Magnon. That the fire in the horn is flickering.

Maybe there is a further and farther realm out there, to which we are all headed, some of us reserving a booking in the penthouse suite while others are destined, this go-around at least, for the mansion's basement. I think my own aspirations in this regard might be to become the groundskeeper, outside as much as possible. I'm remembering now the end of Jim Harrison's 1978 novella, *Legends of the Fall*: "If you are up near Choteau and drive down Ramshorn Road by the ranch, now owned by Alfred's son by his second marriage, you won't get permission to enter. It's a modern efficient operation, but back there in the canyon there are graves that mean something to a few people left on earth: Samuel, Two, Susannah and a little apart Ludlow buried between his true friends, One Stab and Isabel; and a small distance away Decker and Pet. Always alone, apart, somehow solitary, Tristan is buried up in Alberta."

We are not the only ones who are directed this way and that by the swing and pull of neap and full, by the release of first quarter and third quarter, attentive and perhaps addicted to the solace of distance and, less frequently but with greater intensity, to the intimacy and passion of proximity. On full moons, zooplankton rise to the surface as if in the Rapture; oysters spread wider their limestone lips; deer, bedded down, rise as if in a trance no matter what the hour of day or night is when the moon (which is always full, we must remember) is either directly overhead or, curiously, on the other side of this small earth, directly underfoot.

★

Preceding the full solar eclipse of 2018, there was a frenzy of billboards throughout the West, with every lucky farmer whose land fell beneath the dashed line of the eclipse's path across the country—not from east to west, in the style of manifest destiny, but reversing the curse, many hoped, from west to east. It's gone now, as forgotten as KC and the Sunshine Band, a one-hit wonder that people of a certain age henceforth will remember briefly. The arc fell on the just and the unjust, and on the rich and the poor alike. Jackson Hole, south Bozeman; Gooding, Idaho. At the perimeters, overgrazed pastures of dirt, looking like something from Steinbeck's America, wooden towers were erected to serve as billboards a year, even eighteen months, in advance, advertising parking spots and viewing locations. Such was their anticipation that the hand-painted sheets of plywood became sun-faded long before the event, giving the appearance that the eclipse had come and gone many years prior; or that the eclipse itself had aged the signs, delaminated and dilapidated now after having dared profit from such a holy phenomenon. The red spray paint—*Parking, $5.00*—blurring now, wavering like old bloodstains. As the months melted and we were all pulled closer to the day of reckoning, a sweet kind of unification seemed to be happening: the mass of us becoming increasingly aware of the time, date, location—the countdown—with our minds adjusting like crystals in cooling magma, or iron filings attentive to the movement of a powerful magnet, aligning in parallel and then converging from all directions to behold the approaching singularity.

As it will be understood by now, bearing a few pagan tendencies if not quite a willingness to commit fully to the requisite ceremonies and customs of such a sect, I was torn between wanting to take off work and hie down toward the Bitterroot or Gallatin country—only about eight hours, each way by car—versus wanting to behold the phenomenon in my own home valley, reduced or partial though the show would be.

I wanted to feel what my valley felt; wanted to take note of the wind, or breeze, if there was any shift in current, in direction, when the partial darkness fell, as is reported in the Bible for such events "over the land." I wanted to take note of any possible skip or stutter in the pull of gravity beneath my feet, in my home; wanted to hear if the calls of ravens became different, in that darkened hour, and whether the hermit and varied thrushes—crepuscular singers, lovers of the gloom and gloaming—began to sing.

I also, like almost everyone I think, did not want to experience it alone. As if only by witnessing it with another of our kind could it be said to be certain, or 99.999 percent certain.

For weeks and months beforehand, community-service organizations—libraries, notably, and other leftist do-gooders—had been passing out free solar-eclipse sunglasses, distributing them with the same fervor with which school nurses gave children sugar cubes infused with a dose of polio vaccine back in the 1960s. Imagining—fearing—an entire population blinded simultaneously by a single skyward glance, accidental or otherwise, or turned into pillars of salt, or maybe both at the same time, for having dared gaze upon that which they had been warned not to behold directly.

Having procrastinated until the day before, I called around only to discover all supplies had run out weeks earlier. The next best thing, I imagined, might be a welder's helmet, so I drove to town to the hardware store, arriving an hour before closing. There was one helmet left, but it was so expensive! I wanted the free green plastic eyeshades that were given out at the optometrist's offices of my youth. To pay for protecting one's vision? It seemed somehow un-American.

Inspired by necessity, however, I found replacement glass sheets for welder's masks. The internet had actually said that welder's masks were not sufficient—I found this difficult to believe—but to be safe, I bought three sheets, each a little smaller than an index card. And when I peered through them, it was hard to see anything. I guessed that was why welders didn't use three at a time.

The day of, I drove downvalley to the office of the conservation nonprofit I work with. I'd also read it was safer to watch the eclipse reflected in a body of water, rather than staring birdlike directly at the change, so I found a child's blue plastic swimming pool out back and filled it with water.

The staff and I went out into the backyard to wait. There was no morning traffic on the road that runs past our office. We stared at the pool as if awaiting the emergence of the Loch Ness monster; we glanced sidelong now and again, up at the same old sun up in the same old sky. Same old birdsong. The in-between time, in the north country: summer winding down, autumn not yet arrived. Torpor.

It came slowly. There was a blurring, a wavering, that was, to be honest, a little unsettling—more so, I think, than the coming shadow. To have seen a thing one way all one's life, for sixty years, and then to see it, the previously immutable, waver and sprawl a bit—well, what if everything else contained such waver, such wobble?

The edges shimmered in the way that waves of heat rise from highway pavement in deep summer. *Holy shit*, I remember thinking, *it's happening, and on its own time.*

I liked that we all had to be attentive, sitting like schoolchildren, waiting for the teacher to enter the room.

I liked that our office is in an old schoolhouse, back in the woods. A fairy tale.

It didn't get dark so much as fuzzy. There appeared to be a kind of static in the sky, in the air—the visual equivalent of the itchiness or scratchiness of a wool jacket, as if there was a coarser weave of pixels registering on our hungry brain. We glanced again and again up at the sun—once, I saw the black silhouette of a witch on a broom riding the crescent black moon across the face of the sun, west to east—but the hive-mind was right once again. The image was much more distinct when viewed in the children's bathing pool, and in that reflection, the witch disappeared.

I heard a single car approaching. I saw it was the mail carrier, in her white jeep, with her silent flashing wide-load strobe light atop. I got up and walked out to the mailbox to ask if she wanted to come look into the pool, as if into a wishing well. It was hard for me not to think of Sally Swanger's dark water well in the novel and then movie, *Cold Mountain*, where Nicole Kidman, playing Ada Monroe, stares down into its depths and, seeing a swarm of crows, faints. It takes every bit of discipline for me not to tell you what happens subsequently, but it's dark. It's only for your reading and viewing pleasure that I refrain.

The postal lady, amazingly, had not heard about the eclipse.

Our valley is surrounded by high mountain walls with relatively little contact to the world beyond. I asked if she wanted a view.

"Sure," she said. She turned her jeep off and walked with me to the backyard. I imagine driving the same route decade after decade can get a little numbing, even though the scenery is amazing. Always driving, never walking. A hundred mailboxes in a 150-mile round trip, every day—well, six days a week. I handed her the magic panes of dark green glass, told her not to look up without them; told her to look into the pool first, to prepare herself for what she would see above her.

The day was not exceptionally dark, not the pitch-blackness I had envisioned. Instead, its dominant characteristic was stillness—the stillness of hesitation. As if not only were the humans betranced, but everything with a heart that beat or a spirit within, an essence, that pulsed and throbbed.

The mail carrier held the loose little strips of welder's face mask glass carefully—daintily—her smoker's-stained fingertips suddenly elegant, with pinkies lifted, all delicate.

(Back home, I would put the green glass strips in the kitchen drawer, where I knew they would sift to the bottom, never to be seen or used again. I was only mildly tempted to return them for a refund, and I wondered briefly at their provenance. From what beach or ocean floor or mountaintop had the sand been dredged? Did it require a special grade of sand grain? Had an extraordinary furnace of heat been required to process the silica, in order to assist it in blocking, rejecting, one of the most natural and penetrating things in the world, waves of light, relentless and pure, falling—again—on the just and the unjust, with equal democratic vigor, so many years after the initial launch of those waves?)

She stared down into the pool while above us, earth, moon, and sun continued to separate. You could feel it. We were all being returned to our old ways, and it felt . . . good. Not just familiar, but good.

She liked it. She studied the pool—carefully, but also boldly—as if it was for this she had been driving, searching, driving, searching, all her life; looked upward, through the green glass.

In the forest, the birds were making their little late-morning sounds, but—and I acknowledge fully this may only be my interpretation—they seemed to be a little tentative, indecisive.

I stood beneath the static, the strange dim light that was in no way darkness. I felt cleansed somehow, lighter. Not so much forgiven as—cleaner. Childlike.

After a long time of her staring into the pool, I started to wonder if a spell had been cast on the mail carrier; that she might have decided to deliver the mail no more forever. That the little glass plates, unused, would fall loosely from her hands; that she would sit down beside the swimming pool, like the handicapped woman in Andrew Wyeth's portrait *Christina's World* staring up the hill at the big house, and, content now, she would lead a life of such monastic dedication to the baby pool as to forego food—a hunger strike—and, thirsty, would not yet dare to sip from the pool's sun-black water . . .

I wanted to offer to drive the rest of the mail route for her that day. I wondered if we had saved her vision: if, driving upriver, listening to music, she might have noticed the black witch on the black broom riding the black moon across the sun, and, staring at it, had her eyesight so damaged that she could no longer drive the jeep, her freedom from the office, nor would she even be able to sort mail with much accuracy, her demotion to the dreaded desk job resulting in the misdelivery of hundreds and then, over time, thousands of pieces of mail, usually with nondramatic results, though occasionally with such devastating and life-changing consequences that—

I inquired meekly what she thought of it all. She looked up, surprised to see me, I think. The witch was on the back side of the sun now, then free and clear, somewhere invisible out there in all that blue sky. Birdsong did not exactly erupt, but I felt, we all felt, the gears—our gears, as well as the world's—begin to move again. Our office staff began drifting back into the office, back to their work of saving the forests, the mountains, that are our home.

"That was really something," the mail carrier said, looking back down into the water as if waiting for it to reappear. A more crafty entrepreneur than I might have saved the water from the pool, bottle and marketed it, or served it in the local bar after midnight, a Whiskey Ditch, or Witch Whiskey, Maker's with a splash of witch water . . .

She, too, was returning to her old self, but more slowly than the rest of us. Not as if she, like Ada Monroe, had seen the future so much but had been taken back, way back, to some point earlier in her life: young adulthood, or even more distant, back to a time whereupon setting out into each day, one not only expected to see such trippy phenomena but sought them out, on every path, and was often, maybe even usually, thus rewarded.

She walked—shakily, I thought—back to her little white jeep, got in on what has always seemed to me to definitely be the wrong side, and turned on her flashing lights, the amber orbit of them whirling so much more slowly than the strobes of police or ambulance or fire. And she continued on up the road, changed, lightened, leavened, undone, remade, like every thing, and every one of us, 99.999 percent certain about almost anything; and diminished, I think, for that excessive belief, that confidence and security, that assurance and trust. Blinded, even, maybe.

★

I was not done. I sat by the side of the road like a wayfarer, not so much waiting as instead simply decompressing from all I had seen, and the distance I had traveled. The earth to which I had returned.

I felt extraordinarily becalmed. I felt ready to start again. Felt my old self, isolate but seeking to assemble, unify; to find beauty, as Terry Tempest Williams says, in a broken world.

And to disassemble, to seek to stretch wider, if not fully pull apart or unravel the vertical, humming strings of matter—I picture them as being like the bead curtains favored by hippies in the seventies—that physicists tell us represent the percentages and probabilities of reality; to test the almost-certain quality of it, and in so doing, maybe sometimes getting a sniff if not an actual peek at what might be beyond that veil.

I heard a car approaching—other than the mail carrier's jeep, the first one all morning on this strange and bestilled day. It occurred to me that other than our staff and the mail carrier, I'd not seen another human, and that for whomever was driving the approaching vehicle, it had likely been the same.

This world is beautiful but it is never quite finished. One can always push against, sand or polish—or prune or shave—its furthest edges. Without even really knowing what I was doing, I stood, stretched both arms out in front of me in the classic zombie pose, and began walking away from the road, stiff-legged Frankenstein-like, headed for the woods, trapped by the light, as the car and driver zoomed past and, hopefully, if for even just a moment, did a double-take, and wondered at what he or she was seeing or thought they were seeing, before being sucked on farther up the road. As if being drawn toward wherever they were going rather than navigating by free will, desire, hunger: all the shimmering vertical curtains that identify us, get us out of bed in the morning, and keep us moving, moving forward, relentless, if confused.

Horoscopes had promised that everything would be better after the eclipse had passed by. And, for a little while, they were.

The savvy ones did not stay at home like me but went deep into the wilderness, on their own, to nestle on a promontory and wait to be bathed in momentary darkness, with only the edges of all things limned with a corona of fire.

Do they know the answer now, if even only subconsciously, while I still search? When we see, are we really seeing? We know of the 99.999 percent predictability that whatever we are looking at is "real," is true, is a highly probable likelihood of reality—but what does 100 percent look like? Does it even exist? Does it exist in the moon's shadow, as it occasionally falls upon us?

Does the strange planet of us, in those ninety or so minutes of a total eclipse, sag and begin to disassemble or unravel—down to 99.9998 percent, or 97.63 percent—still real, still true, but with stuttering, shuttered images of either a further reality or a further unreality ahead, depending on whether one is looking forward or backward?

I think it feels like the latter; that the past contains a rubbled foundation of fragments and segments of reality, by virtue of their having endured. That in the old darkness, we feel most strongly the calling of our species—the experiment of us. That if we are not yet fully real, we might yet one day make ourselves real. I have to believe the fire in the horn we carry is the will to adhere, will to cohere, amid the shimmering unpredictable. That even when we rage and destroy or disassemble, it is to some degree so that we may then be employed, so to speak, reassembling that which we have pulled apart.

Much of what we behold—that which we have made and woven—is but a dream, surreal and even unreal. As if we have lost our way in the darkness. As if where we began—on the platform of the old stone, at the edge of an old sea, craving light, craving shelter and protection, craving food from the garden, craving craving craving—was the thing, the first moment, that came just after we stepped up from out of the stone. That the old implacable stone is the truth and the light, and that the quivering, shimmering likelihood of us, as we exist or mostly exist right now, but an extreme probability. That those things, the events we call coincidence, wax and wane in almost orderly if not predictable fashion—cascading over one another sometimes like dominoes falling, with such pattern or near pattern that we are alarmed, disturbed, unsettled, and other times with such a wildness, a lack of connection on our movements and our days that we feel, once again, alarmed, startled, disturbed, bereft.

Always without knowing why. Always without being able to see the reason.

We move around in the light, but we cannot yet see. But how we crave, more than ever, those five points of attachment: touch, taste, scent, sight, sound. Come back, rock. Come back, moon.

A DOG IN THE HAND

IT'S A SOMETIMES WONDERFUL and peculiarly Texan afflic-
tion to search for and label things as being the Best or Biggest this
or that, and I was amused to find myself having fallen prey to it.
I felt like a doodlebug falling into an ant lion's trap because I've
been away from Texas for a while, out in the rest of the world,
and I know there are too many people, and too many things—too
many chicken fried steaks, for instance—for anyone or anything
to ever, truly, be the Best.

But I'd been hearing contrary evidence about a bird-dog trainer
outside of the little lost pines town of Rosanky—thirty or so miles
southeast of Austin—all year long, from people in Montana, in
Mexico, and points in between. What I knew about bird dogs
wasn't thimble-worthy, but I get along okay with real dogs and
understand them, even, and I wanted to check out the differences.
I wanted to see if this mythical bird-dog man, Jarrett Thompson,
was sweet or cruel.

What I mean is, I wanted to find out why he was the best.
Speaking of the best, I also wanted to see Elhew Tex, his prize stud
dog, whose great chestiness was displayed in a photo on the cover
of Thompson's Old South Pointer Farms brochure. I remember
staring for long moments at Elhew's obvious greatness when I
first saw that picture: his level gaze, the steadfastness of it, the
stock-still stance of him out in the field, grasses blowing, thunder-
heads building behind him, but far more important things going
on in his noble head. I remember thinking how very much he

looked like Brian Bosworth, the Seattle Seahawks' linebacker. If Jarrett Thompson was the best trainer and his Old South Pointer Farms the best facility, then, I could tell, Elhew Tex was easily the best dog.

★

The long, narrow road through the woods leading to Thompson's farm is canopied, like some tunnel of love. Sunlight comes down in dapples through the big pines, and through the heavy hardwoods, the oaks and hickories. The farm is enclosed by fence so no dogs can escape. To the south not so many miles—fifty or sixty— lies the harsh Texas brush country, where Thompson's customers do most of their quail hunting; they also come from all over the United States, and all over the world, including Spain, Africa, and Australia. Thompson raises and sells his own dogs but also trains other people's. He boards dogs too, but only bird dogs: Brittany spaniels, Weimaraners, Vizslas, English setters, German shorthaired pointers, and English pointers, among others.

Each breed seems to have its own little camp on the farm, and after a long drive down the dusty road, I begin to pass their kennels—dogs leaping, when they see me, in acrobatic twists, entire kennels of all setters, and then, a little farther down the road, also rising and jumping in the sun, all pointers, and then the friendly hound-looking Vizslas, and so on; and finally, at the end, Thompson himself. He's friendly too, and, shaking hands with him, I wonder what the dogs must think of him. He's a sturdy man, smiling, with wheelbarrows full of control all around him, inside him; I can tell that, or want to believe it, just meeting him. Thompson and his wife, Dawn, own and run the farm; there is one other trainer, Bunny Brown, who at first I mistake for a dog when Thompson tells me (we hear yips coming from down in the woods), "That's Bunny and her pups, hunting."

We get in Thompson's truck and work our way toward the

sounds of the training. Various lots have been carved out of the woods to simulate all the possible landscapes a Texas dog might encounter. Thompson is a good talker—two-thirds scientist and one-third storyteller, the best mix—and he begins filling me in right away on what I have missed in the last twenty-five years that he has not, which is how long he's been training dogs.

I want to see if it's cruel or sweet, becoming the best. Thompson is friendly, and from what I've seen of the dogs, they're happy.

The first place we stop is a little grove with a wire box set down on the ground, with all sorts of ropes and cables leading into it from all directions.

"This is a bird launcher," Thompson says. "It's used for launching live birds into the air." Everything can be controlled—everything. Thompson shows me the harness hookup for the dog to keep it from running off when the bird is sprung (by pulling a rope). You can put the dog upwind or downwind of the bird. You can even launch the bird with one hand and shoot the bird, if you wish, and then unhook the dog so he can retrieve it. Every variable can be controlled by ropes and cables; there are little traps like this set up all over the farm so the dogs don't get used to hunting in any one area.

"We use about seven thousand birds a year," says Thompson. A worried look crosses his face then, thinking of the variables, of those things that must be controlled. For instance, he tells me, the trainers sometimes tie a little piece of orange flagging around the birds' legs, to make them easier to find. But the dogs are so amazing, so single-minded, so eager to please—I think of Elhew again—that if the trainers aren't careful, the mind-set of the dogs will slip a notch, and they'll begin pointing not quail, not live birds, but orange flagging, loose and stray bits of it, out in the fields.

We catch up with Bunny, who works all dogs impartially, but whose favorite breed is Brittanies. Bunny enters her own Brittanies in field trials, where the dogs point birds, but hunters do not shoot them. She and Thompson begin to talk to me not so much about the dogs, which are really no problem at all, but about the people. "You can tell 'em from a mile away, what kind of dogs they like," says Thompson. "German-shorthair owners—they're all alike. They're interested in image—they all dress the same. And the Pointer Guys"—Thompson laughs—"they come driving up here in their new Suburban or monster four-wheel-drive truck, big tires, and rattle off the names of past champions, and then get all fond, remembering their best dog of years ago, saying things like, 'There'll never be another one like 'im. . . .'"

"Brittany people, too," says Bunny. "The Brittany people drive up in a station wagon, whole families—a station wagon full of kids—it's their pet, like they're bringing it to summer camp."

"The big problem is that people—owners—don't know how to treat their dogs after they get out of here," says Thompson, "and they don't know what to expect from the various ages of the dog. They'll come in and say stuff to me like, 'I don't understand it, he's slowin' down.' But a twelve-year-old dog is like an eighty-year-old man; of course he's slowing down."

Variables: diet has to change with the older dog. Everything, of course, is always changing. The dogs adapt. It's the people, the owners, who conspire to muck things up.

"Hunters and killers," says Thompson. "When guys come in talking about how many birds they killed—not how many coveys their dogs found, but how many birds the hunters killed—well, I know better than to even bother asking, 'Yeah, but how'd your dog do?'"

What's especially interesting about riding around with Thompson and listening to him talk about these things is that he's as calm as pie, his face as relaxed as can be. He disagrees with hundreds of wrongs, but he's not going to blow a clot, not going to torch the bridges, over them. He's just going to stay back in the woods and do it his way, the right way.

Thompson coached high school boys in football and track for seven years. "I got out of that," he says.

★

They'll train your dog to do anything at Old South Pointer Farms. They run a snake-proofing clinic right before each hunting season, using live defanged rattlesnakes. Thompson's a genius, a mad warlock; he thinks of everything. He uses two rattlesnakes in the clinic—one with rattles still attached, and one without rattles to teach the dog to fear even the scent of rattlesnakes, and not just the sound of their rattles, or the sight of them.

Thompson trains the dogs physically too, not just mentally. The first week of hunting season in Texas is notorious for killing out-of-shape dogs due to heat prostration. So three or four months before each season, Thompson will hook up clients' dogs in harnesses and run them down the road behind fourwheelers, over hill and dale. I think of Tex's chest.

We watch a pretty brown dog, a Vizsla, whip around, snuffling through the grass, hunting a bird Bunny has hidden in the brush (shaking it first, to make it too dizzy to fly away immediately). The dog jumps in the air, flips when she scents the bird, and then freezes hard, crouches down low, having gotten a little too close to the bird, and frightened that she'll flush it.

"Buuurrrd," Bunny says, speaking to the Vizsla the way you might speak to . . . well . . . it's *intimate*. "Buuuurrrrd," she says, and the Vizsla doesn't blink, doesn't move her tail, doesn't do anything at all except blow out a little air through her cheeks, twice, in furious concentration. Bunny moves up and kicks the brush, and the bird rises in an explosion and flies away. The Vizsla doesn't budge. It's her job to wait and see if there are any more. It's as if she scorns the quail that got away. It's the ones that may be remaining that she's after, the ones her hunter may still be able to shoot.

But there are none.

The absence of the shot, the bird flying away, free and clear, and the dog pretending not to care—this hangs between us, slightly. I pet the dog's head. Bunny tells her what a good dog she is. It's hard to separate hunting from killing. The bird being discovered, and pointed, is hunting. It's not good to let the bird always get away, though.

"What about this dog in your brochure?" I ask Thompson, driving across the farm once again, through the woods and back to the kennels. "Tex? Elhew Tex?" I feign nonchalance, ignorance. I can't wait to see him, but to seem too eager would not be at all professional.

"Elhew Tex," says Thompson. "Yes." He doesn't say anything else, and I get that feeling of having walked into the wrong room. The feeling that you know nothing of the world, that everything that goes on in the world is too fast and too far above your head for you to ever play a part in it. You feel like fodder. We ride for a while in silence.

★

"Those pointer guys," Thompson says, "they come in here and say stuff—every time—like, 'Yeah, I've trained many a dog in my time, but I just don't have the time now.' And another thing they say is a dog's a natural. I just don't like the term." It's Thompson's observation—and again, more chagrin, but accepted chagrin—that people don't send their "naturals" to him to be trained. "Those people tend to let that dog slide, and often send to me the poor prospect," Thompson says. These are what he calls "fall-out dogs," which are dogs that become homesick or crack under the pressure of training—dogs that are "offended," he says, just by being around all the other dogs, just by the whole situation.

"I will not accelerate a dog beyond his capabilities," Thompson says—this is what causes a dog to crack—and he's got the first sign of edge in his voice. It's the extraordinary dogs, he believes, that should have the most money and time spent on them, and this, I realize, is why I've come down here. This is why Thompson's the best, and why his dogs are the best. Like the Russians, perhaps, with their athletic programs that identify future star performers at the earliest possible age, Thompson—though he trains all dogs—pulls the stops out on the "extraordinary" ones.

It seems like the perfect time to ask about Tex again, but before I can, Thompson is saying—perhaps thinking of Tex, I imagine—"A dog should be allowed to go to the natural tendency of his ability." It's clear that's how Thompson views himself, and how his operation is run, setting aside the barriers that prevent that dog from moving in the direction of his ability. It's also clear, painfully so, that it's not the dog that sets up these barriers, but the owners.

We're off to look at more dogs then. Bunny's still out in the bush, trying to get more training in before the heat of the day builds up and the dogs must rest until the evening. Thompson wants to show me a dog he's been referring to off and on all morning named Gus—a rather bland name, I think, and I'm a little bit confused by all the attention being given to this small-named dog, Gus—and a little puppy named Scooter.

I know who I really want to see, but I don't know how to bring his name up again without seeming rude. I ride along, working on my nerve. Perhaps he is off with females or something, and they don't want to bother him. Perhaps he's off making money, big money.

Thompson has stories. Not like I'd figured—not stories about dogs. These are all stories about people.

"I hate to see this, man," he says. "These big old macho guys come driving down the road, and bring along the dog's biscuits, his bedding, and bones, and just love on them, before they finally leave. Those kinds of dogs are usually going to be your fallout dogs."

Thompson's favorite story is about this big hunter from Florida—big in the sense that he was a heavy man. A big belly. Jovial. The big guy hugged on his dog—a monster itself, a pointer weighing in at almost eighty pounds—for a while at the moment of parting, and then he took Thompson aside and handed him a gallon of Jack Daniels.

"Now, Thompson," he said, "Old Buck and I each have a glass of whiskey in the evenings after we get through hunting, and I expect y'all to do the same."

Counting boarders and trainers, Old South Farms has up to 250 dogs in the kennels. I like the picture of Thompson and this big Florida dog sitting out there in the evening, drinking their whiskey, and all the other dogs watching. I so enjoyed the story that I forgot to ask whether the dog was any good, and when I got home didn't dare call back and ask—it would have been too much of a letdown to hear the answer be no, or, even more likely, that Thompson didn't remember. One client from West Texas—Odessa—is another favorite story. Thompson forgets the man's name, but the dog was, is, named Ned. It's amazing to me, as the stories come out, how buttersoft the Pointer Guys can be: thick and rich and bumbling with both money and good feeling, like cake icing melting out in the sun, helpless, useless, and sweet, running everywhere.

Ned's owner, an oilman, had a Lear jet and decided he wanted a bird dog—one of the best. But he wanted a friendly dog, one he could keep in the house too, so he came out to Rosanky and picked one out: Ned. It cost him about $2,000 to crank up the jet and fly out there, and he paid $2,500 for Ned. He had Thompson drive him back out to the airport in Austin, where the jet was waiting (oil derrick painted on the tail of the jet, heat currents shimmering off the tarmac, etc.), and he took Ned right up there in the front seat and strapped him in with the shoulder harness, next to the pilot, Ned looking all around and wondering, perhaps, if he would ever hunt again. Thompson says the pilot was rolling his eyes—dog hair on the seat, Ned panting, slobbering—and told Thompson that the seat itself was worth $5,000.

A week later, Thompson got a call from the oilman. "I think Ned's homesick," he said. "Can I fly him home and give him back to you? I'll pay you a thousand dollars to take him. All he does is lie around by the refrigerator," the man said. "I think he misses you, and misses the other dogs. I feel badly."

This isn't the end of them. There are more stories. They roll out of Thompson like a confession. It's easy to see why he lives back in the woods with his dogs, and why he has his farm and the woods fenced: to keep the dogs in, yes, but also to keep the crazies out.

"This big guy—I forget his name, the dog's name was Sarge—was from out of state," says Thompson. "Nice guy—came driving down the road, bringing his dog along, and wanted to see what the farm was like. I had him take me out, just to see what kind of dog Sarge was—what he could do, just what I could expect from him." To see if the dog had what Thompson calls "spark."

"Before we started to do anything, though, the guy asks if he can have just a minute with Sarge, and I say sure, not knowing what's up, and he takes Sarge off a little ways and tells him to sit"—the one thing that Thompson hates to find out bird dogs have learned to do—"and starts talking to him, the way you and I would talk. I'm trying not to listen, and it's making me feel funny, but what this guy's saying, real quietly, is stuff like, 'Okay, Sarge, we drove a long way out here, now I sure hope you're not going to embarrass me,' just talking to him real gentle and kind and quiet. And I'm trying not to listen, but I'm also getting kind of interested, kind of eager to see just what kind of dog this Sarge is, that you can talk to like a person instead of a dog.

"Well, we get out and walk a little ways, and Sarge kind of

cuts up, blows a point, and misses another, and the big guy was just getting all pained, writhing and flinching; every time Sarge messed up, he'd take him aside and have another talk with him— I could still hear him, saying, 'Sarge! You are embarrassing me!'— and finally, when it just wasn't getting any better, the big guy all sweating and upset—asked if he could have some more words with Sarge, alone.

"They got in their truck, and drove down the road a ways—I thought they were leaving—and then they stopped under a shady tree. I could see them sitting there, talking, and after a while the old guy drives back, still looking all pained, and he says to me, 'Sarge and I had a little talk down at the gate, and we decided it'd be best for Sarge to stay here for a while.'"

We're headed for this Gus dog Thompson keeps talking about. Dogs in kennels—intelligent, beautiful-eyed dogs—watch us drive past the kennels shaded by the forest, and every one of these dogs, every single one of them, burns, I think, with this special knowledge, this special ability, that so amazes humans—we who cannot find birds, cannot scent birds, and cannot begin to approach anything (not love, not even breathing, not anything) with the intensity with which the dogs track these birds. And I can see how the Pointer Guys, after being around the dogs for a while, might be in awe of them and treat them as equals, partners, if not superiors; I think that I, too, could find myself, someday, becoming a Pointer Guy.

"Tex died last year," Thompson says, out of the blue, and I glance over at him. Perfect control. There's nothing for me to say. We could be talking about someone's canary. Ashes to ashes.

If I ask another question, will Thompson's lower lip buckle, then tremble? There's that feeling in the air—that terrible, fragile brusqueness. And what can I say? I'm sad, and I feel a horrible sense of loss, and I never even met the great Elhew Tex. I feel like asking, *Well, can't he come back? Don't you have any of his . . . pups?* I do ask this, but Thompson just says "No," and he seems reconciled.

Seems. Is it more control? What is at depth? Does Thompson let himself imagine—or remember—roaming the fields and the woods with his great stud? It's not that I don't dare ask, not that I lack the heart of a cold killer, a professional journalist. It's just that I know I wouldn't get the real answer, the true one.

Tex is in the ground. Thompson has himself under control. I don't want to disrupt any of this—even if I could.

We stop at a kennel and load a young liver-and-white pointer—Gus himself—into the trailer. This dog's physiognomy and demeanor are a far, far cry from the silent nobility of the great Elhew. And then I realize I'm beginning to sound and think like a bona fide Pointer Guy, imbuing a dog I've never met with attributes.

We meet back up with Bunny. She takes another quail from the wire cage welded to the front bumper of her Jeep, and, as before, shakes it up to dizzy it (like a woman shaking dice), and hides it for Gus.

"We have some people come out and hunt on the property sometimes," Thompson says, "guided hunts—and they all want to go hunt with Gus. They never ask if I'm taking them out—all they ever want to know is if they can have Gus. They split up into small groups, and only one group can have Gus. Everybody wants Gus."

Gus—only two years old—once found twenty-two coveys in two hours in South Texas. As I watch him lunge about in his portable kennel, writhing to break free, I realize that this is the Elhew Tex of the future, and I think that maybe I can like his smart brown eyes after all, his broad head (almost like a water snake's), and his width—not the bullish depth of chest Tex had, but a strange, low-to-the-ground, slinking sort of muscled width. And when he hits the ground running—running through flowers, snapping the blossoms off as he races through their midst, blossoms flying everywhere—I know that Gus is a rocket, a stud, and that Elhew can rest in peace.

The wind is a little wrong—we're a little upwind of the bird—and Gus, in his fury, gets in a little too close; he slams on the brakes, his hind end jacking up like a dragster's, and he freezes. And just like that, I am a Pointer Guy.

"Attaboy, Gus," Bunny says. The bird is flushed, flies away. Thompson fires a cap pistol to simulate the miss of a shotgun, and he whistles Gus in.

I remember something my father told me about English pointers. "Craziest dogs in the world," he said.

"See that wire?" Thompson asks, pointing to the heavy-duty diamond-grid wire of the cages, wire so thick that it would not bend even a bit if you hit it as hard as you could with your fist. "We've had pointers chew their way through those cages, they were so anxious to go hunting."

What is it that's in these animals? What kind of juice flows through them that makes them look at the world that way? I'd like to have a little bit of it, whatever it is. Not too much—just a little.

I think about Thompson working with the high school football boys, trying to eke out extra wind sprints from them, quick traps and proper tackles, proper blocks. Thompson won't say if he's a Weimaraner Guy, or a Brittany Guy, or a Pointer Guy, or what; he professes to like all the dogs equally, each on its own merits—his job is to train them, not to like them. But still, one cannot help but wonder. . . .

Sitting next to Gus is a little smiling dog, Blondie, who looks, unbelievably, like Mae West—she's just sitting there grinning, laughing, so happy and eager that we have to let her out, have to let her hunt a bird too. Bunny points out a visiting dog, owned by a city girl in Austin—she lives in an apartment. She will never hunt with her dog, but did not want to deprive the dog of the experience, just once, of hunting, and of knowing what it was like, so she's boarding the dog with Old South for three months and is paying the training fee. Her boyfriend's dog is in the kennel next to it, for the same reason—just so the dogs can have that knowledge, that skill, once.

Is it crueler to learn and then be taken away, than never to hunt at all? We all have slightly varying opinions, and I'm surprised at the strength of my own. It's a crazy world, full of crazy people.

The two dogs I'm speaking of in this instance are, of course, pointers.

I'm looking at Gus, now back in his cage, thinking about the pointers chewing their way through all that wire to get out and go hunting.

"Most bird dogs have enlarged hearts," Thompson says. "They're great athletes, all of them." Too much exercise, too much hunger, too much activity, too much hope, I think; too much everything. I do not see how Thompson can control these dogs' magnificence, but he does.

★

We're off to see Scooter back at the house then—the pup. She's in the prize kennel by herself, the one next to the house. She comes running straight up to me, bounding, wiggling, creeping, tail wagging—pure white with eerie, shining, lightgreen eyes—and I fall in love about as hard as a person can with a dog. She's dancing at my feet, batting me with her dainty paws.

"Come watch this," Thompson says. He's got a rag on a string, tied to the end of a cane pole, and he dances the rag over Scooter's head; she leaves my side and dashes after it, leaping at it, snapping. The rag flutters above her like a ghost.

Thompson lets the rag down to rest in the dust, several yards in front of Scooter.

Scooter slinks down into a crouch, no longer a puppy, and like a snake—that same kind of strange forward motion, moving, but also seeming not to move—she's advancing on the rag, creeping, being drawn toward it by the brute force of however many thousands of years of breeding. She's creeping, slower and slower, sometimes stumbling; at seven weeks, she's still not sure how to walk, but she knows, already, how to hunt, and how to keep her eyes on that rag. It is precisely like watching an infant, still in diapers, working with an adding machine. Something is not right with this picture, something is wrong, and yet there it is: you're watching it, seeing it, and it is real, not magic.

She's tiptoeing, laying one foot out cautiously in front of the other, moving like a snake, and then pointing when she's right over the rag, those strange and beautiful pale-green eyes unblinking on the rag—a million memories racing through her tiny head, remembering things she hasn't even seen yet. And she stands like that, poised over the rag, locked in a perfect point, for two minutes, then three minutes, before she can break out of her trance and pounce.

Thompson tries to snatch the rag away with a quick jerk on the pole, but Scooter's too quick. She's got it in her little jaws, and she's swinging on the end of the pole, growling, playing with it, and she's a puppy once more, and all is soft and well with the world again, and the furiousness, the intensity, has dissolved; it's simply a pleasant cool spring morning.

My knees are weak, though, and my head is buzzing. I did not know such a thing existed in the world. We put Scooter back in her kennel—I carry her over there in my arms, like a baby, and I do not want to set her down—and then we go into the house and have some ice tea with Dawn.

Sitting beneath one of the portraits of Elhew, I have to ask what he was worth, in cold, hard dollars, and Thompson mentions matter-of-factly that some folks over in Japan had offered $12,000, as if the dog were some aging major-league baseball player.

Thompson may still be feeling a little tense-headed about Elhew, a little tightthroated—how could anyone not?—but he displays nothing, and if he feels anything, it's a secret, a perfectly kept secret.

I think about what a tiny amount of money $12,000 is for an athlete such as Tex, or Gus, or Scooter. Because let me tell you, these dogs are better at what they do than any player ever was, and, I believe, more entertaining. There's no comparison to me between watching some million-dollar-a-year slugger poke a ball over a fence versus watching the life-and-death mystery of one of these dogs ferreting out that tiniest, most hidden, most explosive bird, slamming on the brakes when it catches the scent, and then locking in on the point with a certainty you couldn't have previously believed existed in the world.

I don't really understand the economics of it—the low cost of pure pleasure—but of course there is much else I don't understand also, and I simply marvel at it, and I am surprised. It is to be seen, before leaving this earth, these dogs and their magic; it simply must be seen.

Dawn picks up the infinitely lovable Scooter as she and Thompson are walking me to my truck, and she squeezes her, holds her; much licking of the face, chewing of the earlobe.

"Yes, yes, Scooter," Dawn coos to the licking pup. "You're going to be Gus's wife someday, aren't you?"

Those eerie green eyes. How many birds will this dog point in her life? How many will be flushed, their secrets released, told upon, rocketing from the brush, only to fall? Such a strange, beautiful shade of green.

Gus and Scooter: happy, happy dogs, and damned good at what they do. Mr. and Mrs. Right. Such joy. Nothing, or no one, has ever enjoyed something the way Gus and Scooter enjoy freezing when that scent hits them. It's the most magical thing I've ever seen. Wishing them many puppies. Many happy puppies.

The quail? All they know is to flee.

It's a hard world out there. Fury, and excellence, abound.

THE FARM

IT WAS STILL THE END of winter at our home in northern
Montana, but down in south Texas in April, at my father's farm,
it was full-bore spring. It was a joy to me to realize that Lowry,
just turned three, would now have the colors and sights of this
place lodged in at least her subconscious, and that Mary Katherine, just turned six, was old enough to begin doing some serious
remembering.

Some children, of course, hold on to odd-shaped bits and
pieces of memory from a much earlier age, but around the ages of
six and seven, nearly everything can be retained—or at least that
was how it worked for me when I was a child.

It was like a kind of freedom, a kind of second welcoming her
into the world. Now when I am an old man I will be able to say to
her, "Remember when . . ." and she will remember. We had flown
to Austin, rented a car, visited B.J., and then driven down into
the brush country and toward the live oaks and dunes in braided
twists some fifty miles inland, to the farm.

As we drove, Elizabeth and I talked and watched the late-day
sunlight stretch across the green fields. The girls slept in the back
seat, tired from their travels. So much joy do they bring me that
sometimes I wonder if, since my mother is no longer here to love
and know them, I'll carry also her share, having inherited it pre-
maturely. For a fact, this joy seems almost too large. I think maybe
that is what is happening sometimes, at certain moments. I glance
at them and love them fully and deeply, but then a second wave

or wash comes in over that one, as if she is watching them over my shoulder.

It used to give me a bittersweet feeling, but now I'm not sure what the word for it is. Gratitude: to the girls, of course, but also to my mother.

They woke when we stopped to open the gate. We drove through and closed the gate behind us, and because we could not wait to get out and walk, we parked the car there and decided to walk instead of drive the rest of the way to the farmhouse. We walked in the late-day light, the last light, down the white sandy winding road, beneath the moss-hung limbs of the enormous live oaks—trees that are five and six hundred years old. It's so strange, the way there will be certain stretches of time, certain moments, when for a little while it will feel exactly as if I am walking in her every footstep—as if I am her in that moment, set back in time—and enjoying that moment as I know she must have enjoyed it, or one like it, decades earlier.

Buttercups, wine-cups, and black-eyed Susans, Before we had taken ten steps, Lowry and Mary Katherine each had picked double-fistful bouquets and had braided flowers into their hair. Another ten steps took us across the culvert that ran beneath the road. There was water standing in the culvert and in the receding little ponds on either side of the road, and as we approached, a thousand little frogs went splashing into that muddy water.

"Frog alert, frog alert!" we cried, and ran down to mud's edge to try to catch one, but there were too many, zigzagging in too many directions; you couldn't focus, couldn't chase just one. There were so many frogs in the air at any one time that occasionally they were having midair collisions. The mud around the shoreline of their fast-disappearing pond glistened, so fast was the water evaporating, and the mud was hieroglyphed with the handprints of what might have been armies of raccoons, though it also could have been the tracks of one very unsuccessful raccoon.

We finally caught one of the little frogs and examined it, the gray-brown back that was so much the color of the mud, and the pearl-white underbelly.

Into the farmhouse she loved so much—she had lived in it, and loved it, for only a few years before she fell ill, but she had loved it so fully in that time that I still cannot step into it without feeling that remnant love of place. And it is thin substitute for her absence, but with the exception of my own blood in my veins, and memories, it is all there is, and I am grateful for it.

Elizabeth wanted to go for a run in the last wedge of light—after the long Montana winter we were nearly delirious with the gift of these longer days—and so she laced up her running shoes and went on back up the road at a trot. Mary Katherine wanted to go fishing in the stock tank, so we rigged up a line and went off toward the pond, following the winding sand road and walking beneath those old trees.

We stood on the levee and cast out at the ring of flat water. Turtle heads appeared in the center of the lake, tipped like little sticks, to observe us. In the clear water of the shallows we could see the giant Chinese grass carp, fifteen pounds each and seemingly as large as horses striding just beneath the surface, cruising; my parents had put them there when they first built the pond as a means of keeping algae from overtaking the pond. The carp are hybrids, so they can't reproduce, though it's rumored they can live to be a hundred years old—and because the carp are strictly vegetarians, there was no chance of them striking at our spinnerbait. It was strange, though, watching the giant fish circle the pond so slowly, their dorsal fins sometimes cresting the surface like sharks, and knowing that we were fishing for something else, something deeper.

On the far side of the pond, a big fish leapt—not a carp, but a bass. We cast to it for a while in the gathering dusk, but I was hoping that we wouldn't catch it. It's good for the girls to learn that you don't get something every time you go out, or right away.

A water moccasin swam past, its beautifully ugly wedge of head so alarming to our instincts that it seemed almost a mild form of hypnosis—as did the eerie, elegant, S-wake of its thick body moving across the surface.

Floating on the pond were four-leaf clovers my parents had planted—a special variety in which every one of them had four leaves—and we stopped fishing for a moment and picked some for friends. Across the field, across the rise, we could see the cattle trotting in front of the blood-red sun, running from something, and in that wavering red light, and across the copper-fading visage of the pasture, it looked like some scene from the wilderness of Africa, a vast herd of wildebeest. The cattle passed from view, and then a few moments later we saw the silhouette of Elizabeth jogging behind them, along the crest of the rise. And across the distance we watched her run in that Mars-red light, the sun behind her, as seven years ago at our small wedding I had sat by this same pond with my mother and watched Elizabeth and my father ride horses across the face of that sun.

We resumed casting. A mockingbird flew up and landed in the little weesatche tree next to us, not five hundred yards away, and as the sun's fireball sank as if into an ocean, the mockingbird began singing the most beautiful song. It was some intricate melody that, in the bluing of dusk and then the true darkness, was one of the most beautiful songs I'd ever heard, a serenade.

"Sing back to him," I told Lowry, and so she did; she sang her alphabet song there in the darkness, her *Now I noma A-B-C's— next time you can sing with me.*

Finally it was true dark—the mockingbird was still singing— and we headed back toward the house. We saw a shuffling little object, some humped small creature, shambling down the sand road in front of us, and I cried, "Armadillo! Chase him!"

We set out after him in full sprint, and we were almost even with him—he was running in weaves through the trees—when I noticed the white stripe running down his back and was able. barely in time, to shout, "Skunk! Get back!"

Perhaps it was the four-leaf clovers. The skunk went his way and we, ours. I had the strangest thought in my relief, however. I found myself wondering how—had we been sprayed—the girls would have thought of me afterward, growing up. What if they grew up to be storytellers? What kind of mirth would they have with that—recounting, for the rest of their adult days, the time their father told them to chase and catch a skunk?

How lucky they were, by fluke, to remain in normalcy and to escape unsprayed, untraumatized; and how lucky I was, by the matter of a few feet, to not have such identity fastened to me by my children with the permanence of myth.

I remembered the time when I was about Mary Katherine's age, when my cousin Randy was sprayed by a skunk. It was right around Christmas. We were all gathered up at Grandma and Granddaddy Bass's in Fort Worth: my parents, brothers, and myself; Aunt Lee, Uncle Jimmy, and my cousins. I had already gone to bed—I think it was Christmas Eve—but Randy, being a few years older, was allowed to go down to the creek to check his troutlines and his Havahart trap one more time.

I had just gone to sleep when I awoke to the impression that all the doors in the house had been blown wide open by some awful force. All of the adults had just let out a collective roar, and then there were gasps and more groans and my uncle's voice, above all others: "Randy, get out of the house!"

Then the smell hit me. Even in the back room, it was stout. I hadn't known that an odor could be that powerful. It seemed it could levitate the house. It certainly levitated the people in the house.

When I went out to ask what all was going on, I seem to recall a furious, sputtering inarticulation on the part of the grown-ups, until finally—or this is how I remember it—they shouted, "*Randy!*"

Thirty-plus years later the girls and I let the skunk travel on his way, and we went on, still sweet-smelling. We could see the glow of the farmhouse through the woods and were striking toward it, holding hands and walking carefully in the darkness to avoid stepping on any skunks, when I saw a firefly blink once, then twice, in the distance.

The girls had never seen fireflies before. I am not sure they had even known such creatures existed.

For the next hour we chased them through the meadow, trying to catch just one. It seemed a harder task than I remembered from my own childhood—I remembered filling entire lantern bottles with them—and I figured that might be because it was still early in the spring and they were not yet blinking with full authority or intensity. We'd see only an individual blinking, and always at some great distance.

We'd break into a run, hoping to arrive there before the blink faded, but they were always a little too far away, and their luminescence lasted only a few seconds. We would leap at that last instant, toward the always-ascending fading glow of gold—leaping with cupped hands and blind faith toward some imagined, calculated place ahead of us where we believed their path would take them. We would open our hands cautiously then, in the silver moonlight, to see if, like a miracle—plucking a star from the sky—we had succeeded in blind-snaring one.

As beautiful as the on-again, off-again drifting missives of the fireflies was the seamlessness with which Mary Katherine accepted unquestioningly the marvel of such an existence. As if secure almost to the point of nonchalance, or at least pure or unexamined wonder, that yes, of course, this was the way all silver-moon nights were meant to be passed, running and laughing and leaping with great earnestness for drifting, low stars blinking against the background of fixed, higher stars.

Eventually we caught one. And one was enough. We went through the time-honored ritual of putting it in a glass jar and punching air holes in the top. We took it inside the house and turned off all the lights. That simple, phenomenal, marvelous miracle—so easy to behold—as old familiar things left us, replaced by a newness in the world. The heck with electricity, or flashlights. Yes. This is the world my daughters deserve. This is the right world for them.

Later that night, after a supper cooked out on the grill and after the girls were asleep (dreaming, I hope, of leaping), Elizabeth and I went for a long walk in the moonlight. The brightest, most severe platinum light I have ever seen; a glare of intense silver-blue light.

The next day we all went fishing. It was windy, and Elizabeth's straw sun hat blew off and landed right-side up on the pond. We watched it sail quickly, without sinking, all the way across the little lake. Mary Katherine ran around to the other side of the lake and was there to fish it out with a stick when it arrived. She ran it back to Elizabeth, who put it back on and tied it tighter this time.

The joy of children catching fish—there's nothing like it. Most of the few fish we were catching were too small, and we kept throwing them back. Lowry's pink skin, her bright blonde hair in that beautiful spring sun. A hundred feet of snow, it seemed, back home in Montana, though this was once my home, and it's a wonderful feeling to be able to come back to a place that you have left and to feel that place welcome you back, and to feel your affection for it undiminished across time.

That night, after our fish fry, I took Mary Katherine into town for an ice cream cone; Lowry had already fallen asleep. I get so used to doing things with them together that I have to remember this, to always be there to spend some time alone with each of them. The special quality or nature of that is as unique as the unique quality of sunlight early in the spring, seen dappled through a new green canopy of emerging leaves, or in the late fall, when the light lies down soft and long again after the harsh summer.

It was dusk again and nighthawks were huddled along the edges of the white-sand roads as we drove slowly beneath the arched limbs of more old live oaks. Fireflies were out in the meadows again and we rode with the windows down to feel the cool night air. The radio was playing very quietly—a jazz special, with the music of Sonny Rollins and Louie Armstrong—and I knew by the way Mary Katherine rode silently, happily, that she had never heard such music before.

ADVENTURES WITH A TEXAS NATURALIST

Roy Bedichek

ALMOST ANY TEXAN, and any writer or reader or naturalist interested in that region, has heard of the literary cornerstone laid down there by J. Frank Dobie, Walter Prescott Webb, and Roy Bedichek in the early and middle part of the last century. The three old boys were friends. I understand they drank whiskey and sometimes ate meat and lolled around campfires and got all passionate about nearly everything, but always about art and about nature; about Shakespeare and warblers, about Odysseus and catfish. They hung out together in what I believe is one of the very sweetest and best parts of the state, the hill country, during what was a sweet and good, if bittersweet, time in that country's natural history.

Although the country and its species had been pretty much discovered and explored and named up, they had not yet been bruised irreparably by the brutish impositions of fragmentation and destruction. You could still hold out hope, even belief, that a lone black jaguar might occasionally wander the remote stretches of the Pedernales. It was not uncommon to know someone who had known the Comanches, or to lay eyes upon an old man or woman who had laid eyes upon the last free herds of bison. There were still wolves in Texas then—red wolves, Mexican lobos, and gray wolves, and you could still find people who had come across grizzlies in West Texas.

These things—this bedrock wilderness, and bedrock markers of a region's cultural as well as natural identity—had vanished only so recently that they were still right at the edge of time and being; even if they were gone, their presence was still felt, was still resonant. There was not the yellowing-newspaper quality to these things that there is now. These things had been gone only so recently that perhaps it even seemed possible they might come back any day.

I knew more about Dobie and Webb than I did Bedichek. Dobie's importance to the state of knowledge in Texas—especially folklore—is well documented, well preserved as is Webb's, due mostly to Webb's landmark work, *The Great Plains*. It's this third dead white male, however—Bedichek—who in my opinion seems less preserved, less known and read, and this represents a real loss, not just to present and future Texans, but to the world-wide community of readers. His book, *Adventures with a Texas Naturalist*, is, I hope and believe, timeless.

Born in the nineteenth century, Bedichek created work that will step across and into the twenty-first. It chronicles what was there in the hill country at that time, during a single year of his musing and literary stock-gathering. But beyond the work's simple value as data-load (the commonality of Vermilion Flycatchers back then, the presence and habits of golden-cheeked warblers, etc.), the book stands to enrich us with the clear passion of itself. To me it has as much strength and message, if not readership, as Leopold's *A Stand County Almanac* or Thoreau's *Walden*.

One of the things that's most amazing and encouraging to me is how gleefully politically incorrect Bedichek was, even back then—not for the sake of incorrectness itself, but for the simple sake of passion and free thinking.

Muir and Thoreau wrote out of an Emersonian tradition where

God is often the face of Nature. They wrote in a time and country where Bierstadt's glory sunsets were accepted as being nothing other than the back door into Heaven. Because of this favorable milieu, their passionate writing, while still the best of its kind, carries to me a bit of the scent of the free glide, the easy way home. Writers such as Muir and Thoreau were visionaries, true, and two of the most original thinkers our country has ever had—but still, they were working in fairly advantageous intellectual environments.

When Bedichek did his free thinking, and embraced just as unabashedly as Muir and Thoreau the golden face of Nature-as-God, the milieu for this kind of thing was much harsher. There was a backlash of objective scientism going on that the time—a reaction that lasts to this day. It was being taught that you can't be a good scientist or naturalist if you love or have passion for your subject. That's finally starting to change, thank goodness, as scientists are remembering that science is about discovery, and that the best discoveries come out of hunger, and that there is a greater danger in being too distanced from one's subject than being too close—and that above all, we're human, and we can't repress our essence, our passions, anyway. But when Bedichek was watching and writing about and trying to make sense of nature (or rather, trying to understand the sense already in nature), that was not the way people—especially scientists—thought.

There was at that time much ridiculing going about the "Nature Fakers"—people who waxed poetic, who let their hearts burn aflame with the wild, their hearts bursting into poetic incandescence at the slightest breeze. The glint of sun off a single dragonfly's wings might be enough to send them into a paroxysm of nature's embrace and proclamations to Heaven's miracles.

To be sure, quite a bit of nature-fakery was going on at this time—people pretending to have feelings as insights they didn't really have—but in our typically American way, anyone who got anywhere near that stereotype was lumped in as a nature-faker and was dismissed as being passionate and therefore meaningless.

None of this evidently meant anything to Bedichek. He just wrote his heart out and spoke that strong double-dose mix of passion and intellect, unafraid or unconcerned of who might lump him where. Which is of course why, as they say in academic circles, he has survived.

So he was not timid or cowardly in his admissions of love for the land; he was not afraid to observe and then propose that geese, for example, are capable of feeling joy and exhilaration.

The irony is that Bedichek was such a good, and sorely missed, naturalist. He seemed to have an instinct as to when to be an artist—when to open his heart, his passions, his emotions, to take flight—and when to walk the steady line and be the good scientist, to simply take good notes, gather good data.

He was meticulous about tracking down the sources and thought patterns that gave rise to folklore and dissecting them all the way to their essence in order to give a proper evaluation. He observed and studied everything, it seems, but especially the birds, from the apparently random cawing of crows to the perching habits of goldfinches versus those of sparrows. Early in his book, he records with macabre, unblinking precision the ancient act of a snake swallowing a frog. Bedichek the artist knows how to start a good story: "One afternoon a distress-croak attracted my attention and, looking about a bit, I found in a patch of weeds near the pond a young frog struggling to free himself from a snake . . ."

But then, like the good scientist, Bedichek remembers to measure, to quantify the frog, before it's gone down the gullet of the pencil-thin snake: "an inch across the shoulders, while his forelegs added another inch."

I believe Bedichek's strength was his own wild heart; his solitary, educated, mockingbird's heart—a bird he clearly identified with (all right, I'll say it—a bird he clearly loved). A bird that could one moment break into beautiful song, and at the next minute turn fierce. A bird with a double dose of passion. For all his sweet singing and gentle nature, Bedichek knew when and how to swoop as well, as in this attack on big agriculture and chicken farms:

> The science which is principally concerned with commercial profit has an awful case of big-head and has become intolerant of any suggestion coming from the laity. If, with no array of statistics, no graphs, none of the parade or paraphernalia of research, you even suggest that this science might have overlooked something, you are set down as an ignoramus: and if you introduce any humanitarian consideration, you are catalogued not only as an ignoramus, but a slushy sentimentalist . . .
>
> This is true, of course, only if science in whose results profit is a stake. There is another science, as everyone knows, of quite different character and outlook. The man who tries to make fun of Science is a fool. Science is sacrosanct, but scientists are not; and especially not are those scientists who have been bitten by the commercial worm and tend sometimes to prostitute science by calling it "applied." These may profess science in season and out, and may even be professors of science, but they are guilty of the same kind of desecration which gave English the name "profane." A certain kind of science defends cigarette-smoking, whiskey-drinking, patent-medicine fakes, adulterated foods, low valuations for tax purposes of corporate assets, and the like.

For Bedichek, pure science was beautiful to the point of holiness, as was literature, as was nature, as was . . . perhaps everything.

Did I say he had a double dose? Make it a triple. Make it unlimited.

Another thing I admire about Bedichek, and a thing of great

value that I think he has to offer us, is his perception of the relationship between humans and nature. For so many of the Romantics before him, human beings were cut off from nature, estranged forever. This was not so for Bedichek. But if humankind was not out on the perimeter, neither was it in the very center. To Bedichek's informed view, a human was pretty small in the universe—a little larger than a snail or an insect, but not much, and not always. He writes here of walking through a field in which a flock of swallows appears before him:

> The birds swarmed about me, darting uncomfortably close to my head in their ambition to be on really intimate terms with an animal of another species. When I stopped, they stopped; when I moved on, they played along with me. I was flattered by this attention, but a prosaic explanation of it arose when I noticed that my feet moving in the high grass started thousands of small, and to my eyes, almost invisible insects flying over the bluff. Since the swallow is not equipped to go after his insects in the grass, he welcomes assistance from any lumbering, bigfooted land animal that happens to come along, including man.

A more beautiful example of Bedichek's view of the wreath, the weave, of humans and nature—a breathtaking passage of nature writing, or heart writing—occurs when a woman in charge of a nursing home calls to ask for Bedichek's help. One of her patients can't sleep at night, she explains, for worrying about a bird's call—a bird the old man can't identify. The old man can't walk and can barely talk, but he hears that bird call (tries unsuccessfully to imitate it), and it's tormenting him.

Bedichek decides to help the old man:

> I saw that he was overexerting himself, so I left him, promising to return next morning and try to identify the call. He

scrawled on a piece of paper 'if sunny and still,' which indicated to me that he was enough of a naturalist to have noted that the call was associated with the weather, as is the case with so many birdcalls.

It was sunny and bright the next morning, quite warm for the twenty-second of February. I had been sitting by his bed only a little while, when he held up a hand shaking like a leaf in the wind and said with evident excitement, 'There it is!' I listened but heard nothing. His hand went up again, but still I heard nothing. Then with great effort he pointed toward a south window, and I leaned out, listening, and sure enough, there it was faint and far away, but distinct enough to be identified.

Bedichek returns frequently to visit the old man, who grows stronger in the spring. They go for field trips together. (Bedichek notices once that as the old man drifts off to sleep, the bird they were listening to came right to the window, "giving forth his crowing call right in our ears.")

It turns out the old man was "a botanist who felt deeply the living presence in nature. He was interested not only in mechanism, but also in the mysterious force that uses mechanism for its occult purposes."

This short, brilliant burst of writing illuminates nearly the whole of two human lives, and the human condition, in less than three pages. It ends with Bedichek's memory of the old man, which is stirred every time he hears that one specific bird's call—the old man "trembling with palsy on the brink of the grave but still, like a youth, in love with sun and flowers and birds and generally with the out-of-doors."

A man not estranged on the lonely perimeter and not in the center, but instead comfortably and generally with nature, all mixed up in the weave of the sun, the flowers, the swallows, the insects, and the men, women, and children—that was Bedichek's view. Some days, many days, a single birdsong is larger than any of us will ever be in a hundred years of living.

Barry Lopez has said that generosity is an act of courage, and I think it can also be said that restraint is a form of strength. I think one of the most remarkable instances of this cool, restrained strength is shown to us in a section where Bedichek is out roaming a 14,000-acre forest in East Texas, along the Neches River—"an island of life in the midst of a weary land devastated by unscientific cultivation which followed in the wake of the insatiable sawmills."

While wandering through the woods, then leaving the woods and walking through cutover pastures where scrawny cows struggled to stay alive, Bedichek observes that in this ragged clear-cut land, "the big lumber interests had moved out years before and were succeeded here by small ranchers who were mere gleaners, picking up crumbs after the rich and ancient life of the country had been ravished."

In the midst of this desolation, Bedichek happens upon an amazing thing of almost Biblical beauty and mysticism. The kind of discovery, the kind of revelation, that—no discredit of disrespect intended—Muir or Thoreau would have gone ape over, would surely have written on in tumultuous ecstasy; a thing upon which they would surely have spent themselves.

It's a monstrous wind-felled sweetgum tree, and Bedichek approaches it almost cautiously, one feels, as he might approach a fallen soldier—this lone giant out in the scabrous middle of the wasteland.

As he nears the huge tree, Bedichek hears a strange humming, a vibrating coming from the shell of the tree itself. There's a tangle of flowers swarming the rotting tree—"masses of deep purple *tradescantia* mingled with red mallow in full bloom," and sunflowers, coneflowers, bellflowers, too. Hovering over all these flowers are dozens of hummingbirds, but that wasn't the only life that was seething within the dead tree.

The deep bass of the rubythroats, almost too low at times to hear at all, was accompanied by a humming in a higher pitch, heard only on nearer approach, coming from numerous honeybees, which had also discovered this bonanza. A few highly colored butterflies associating with many drab ones were about also—some perched on exposed twigs, slowly opening and closing their gorgeous wings, some feeding, some flitting about.

The massive corpse of this tree was disintegrating amid a display of life's more lively and colorful expressions: bees, butterflies, hummingbirds and flowers. Of course, less conspicuous life was thriving therein, but I can't find that I made any note of it. I rarely notice an insect until it is in the bill of a bird, and then I want to know all about it.

Any of the rest of us—almost any writer of any kind—would surely have been tempted to pause and muse something horrible such as, "and I stopped and thought how . . . etc., etc."

Bedichek, however, just watches and listens to the seething giant tree, and then keeps walking.

But perhaps it's no surprise that Bedichek was capable of such moments of understated artistic grace. I feel certain Bedichek would agree that the patterns and theories of art, in their greatest strengths and executions, mimic those of nature. Where Bedichek writes here of nature's patterns, he could just as easily be lecturing to a class on the dynamics of the short story of the novel:

This is all a way of life worked out as a part of nature's plan. As in an individual life, there is a principal of unity and symmetry always active, always harmonizing and constraining anarchic forces, bringing them into due subordination, so in the whole of nature, as diverse and contradictory as it may appear in any partial view, there is a 'dark, inscrutable workmanship that reconciles discordant elements.'

And here, where Bedichek speaks of nature, once again he could be speaking of art:

Alliances, mutual dependencies, parasitisms, preyer and preyed-upon. Linkages joining into one chain a dozen widely differentiated forms, and other relationships amazingly intricate weave all life, animal and vegetable, into the unity of one vast organism. It is exciting, especially when we of more mystical inclinations fancy we feel a pulse of sympathy beating through it all.

The pattern of life, and of art—Bedichek ultimately saw it all in nature and realized, half a century ahead of its peak (let us hope!), the consequences to societies who stepped away from those patterns of logic. How it would crush him, though probably not surprise him, to see the dangerous path we have taken, and how the loss of land ties—and subsequently, land ethic— is making us into a country of brute ignoramuses, barely able to speak the language in which we were once raised: the language of the naturalist.

"This deprivation has come on so gradually that we fail to realize the greater tragedy of it," he writes. Not only do human relationships break down as a result of our stepping out of our biological (and hence moral and social) pattern of being, "but at the same time we are divorced from other species with which we have enjoyed intimacy for ages." In this passage we hear the echo of his contemporaries, Aldo Leopold and D. H. Lawrence.

Divorced, hell. We divorced the land, but that wasn't enough. Now we're coming back to *kill* it. What would Bedichek think? Surely he'd be mad—as in driven crazy. He was witness to the leading edge of so many of Texas's losses. Bedichek lived and wrote just after the grizzly, lobo and bison were gone, and as the golden eagle, ivory-billed woodpecker, and pileated woodpecker were on the ropes. But how could he have imagined that it would not end there, this unraveling of the beautiful weave—that the list of the lost would not end with the great and the powerful, the largest of the birds and mammals, but would extend all the way down? What would he make of the fact that today in Texas, once ubiquitous species such as alligator snapping turtles and horned toads have gone to a federally endangered listing in only a few years?

But perhaps he saw it coming. At least he didn't have to stick around to witness more of it than he did. Even back then, though, there were moments when his wise and gentle observations fell away and revealed, or created, a range at the powerlessness against this acceleration of loss, the totality of it. Witness this lament, this indictment of those who failed to either act for themselves or for the future, at a time when the unraveling *must* be stopped:

> ... various voluntary organizations make up the only nuclei of resistance to what is often ignorant and indiscriminate persecution (of the natural world). The great unorganized mass of people who simply love wild creatures and glory in the vast variety of nature, and consider the extinction of any species of life a catastrophe of major proportions—in short, people who believe that the educative power of nature is almost, if not quite, indispensable to the forming of a genuinely moral character—these have no machinery for effective action and few organs of protest, even.

This is obviously a gentleman's way of saying he wanted to rip someone's lungs out.

We do have organs of protest, however. Unfortunately, Bedichek was one of them, and he's gone. *Adventures with A Texas Naturalist* remains.

Leopold is much read and well known, and deservedly so.

Because the two men were naturalists—men who spend time on the land—they could ring the alarm with eerily similar perceptions while working in different territories.

"The land is one organism," Leopold was writing, "its parts, like our own parts, compete with each other and cooperate with each other. . . . If the land mechanism as a whole is good, then every part is good, whether we understand it or not. . . . To keep every cog and wheel intact is the first precaution of intelligent tinkering..."

Around the same time, Bedichek was trying to teach us the same thing

"Each natural object," he wrote, "the fixed star or the 'unenduring cloud,' merges itself in a frame from which it cannot be torn without loss. There is no insulated spot in nature, but each link is linked, and it is through the interminable linkage that the active principle of the ancient philosophers and the modern nature poets circulates, intelligent observation is not an isolating process, but an unfolding."

"All nature is hitched together," Thoreau tried to teach us over a hundred and fifty years ago: an easy lesson that this rich continent's indigenous people understood from childhood.

We cannot keep ignoring these lessons, cannot keep failing to learn, with impunity. The land and its lessons, its wholeheartedness, will soon be gone, and books such as *Adventures with a Texas Naturalist*, and their lessons, will fall away to dust, and things will become so dire and confused that we won't even know what it is we don't know.

How brave Bedichek was to merge the scientist with the poet—day with night—and how powerful the alchemy of that alliance. He writes with a loving compassion for the crooked, haggard, iron-tough hackberry tree, admiring without reservation the tree's ability to "fight every inch of its life in an inhospitable environment." Bedichek notes with glee the wildness with which the hackberry's passionate roots seek out water and of how, if trapped in a city, the hackberry's roots will "seek out leaks in water piped and crowd into them like thirsty cows about a watering trough. They have a nose for sewer pipes also and wreck them." One can almost hear Bedichek cackle at the tree's inability to conform to our concept of linear neatness, which is the antithesis of wilderness.

"Even in the act of dying, especially in domestication, the hackberry's habit is unpleasant and inconvenient," he all but crows. "It dies by inches and sheds its corpse about piecemeal for several years. When its days are done, I like a tree, like little dog Rover in the nursery rhyme, to die all over."

Clearly, Bedichek had an affinity for this rough species, and for the shared passion he and the tree held for the mysteries of this rugged piece of country. "Lately I saw a bulldozer uproot a hackberry tree two feet in diameter and at least fifty feet tall," he wrote. "Directly beneath the trunk, as the tree fell over, I saw a great fragment of limestone clutched in a mass of roots. This stone was a foot thick and three feet square. In its natural position the trunk of the tree had stood directly over the stone, and the encompassing roots clung with such tenacity that when the tree was pushed over, the great stone was torn from its bed. The hackberry," Bedichek wrote, "loves the limestone."

Bedichek refers to the hackberry as a "John-the-Baptist of a tree" that breaks up the rocky land as a pioneer for others, and one cannot help but make the short leap to the work of naturalists and writers such as Dobie, Webb, and John Graves, who have helped break up the rocky reefs of ignorance in their attempts to save some of Texas's remaining wildness—and of the work of other naturalists and woods-walkers who, like the hackberry, love the land and cling to it.

When Bedichek writes at the end of this book about encountering the eighty-six-year-old man chopping cedar deep in the woods, he marvels at the ancient ax-man's independence, his fierce inability to remove himself from a physical engagement with the land. "Seventy-six years cutting cedar!" Bedichek exclaims. "This is the pioneer philosophy of being up and doing, of marching on to the end of the row, of never quitting. It is the gospel of salvation by work." This strength, this force of human spirit, which can be so heroic in the individual, can also be the same thing that, misdirected or *en masse*, can be so deadly.

What once seemed a benefit to us as a species—this ferocity of linear drive, the ability to muscle straight on, straight ahead, without bogging down with time-consuming consideration for the things surrounding us—the seemingly extraneous things such as ivory-bills and grizzlies—is now the very thing that is causing us, as a species, to wobble and teeter; the proof finally revealing itself, as an echo to writer's works such as Bedichek's, that it is all hitched together.

We've forged ahead with the unblinking fury of the lifelong cedar-chopper. For the most part, we've ignored every other part of the whole, other than ourselves. And now we, and our whole system around and within us, are dying piecemeal, like a hackberry in the city.

"Life is delicate but infinitely inventive and, armed with a feather, crushes stones that happen to be in its way," writes Bedichek.

Adventures with a Texas Naturalist is both a stone and a feather. Reading it, we are being given another chance to listen.

TOLEDO BEND

THE LAKE HAD ONLY BEEN FLOODED for eighteen years when I first came to it in 1976, the year of the bicentennial. The trip was my high school graduation gift. My father and I stayed a couple of nights in a fish camp cabin, the famous Fin and Feathers, which at that time was not quite so upscale. We hired a guide and went out and caught some bass—not hogs, but decent ones, though what I remember from that trip is the giant bream we caught on cane poles from a little rowboat later in the day, after we had finished bass fishing. We were both young—it astounds me to realize my father then was only forty-two—and we had nothing but energy. Part of it was our youth and mind-set—*take big bites from life*—but part of it was the 1970s in Texas, which was probably kind of like the 1960s everywhere else, carried along by the fountainhead of the music that is now called classic rock, and by the oil boom, which totally empowered an already vigorous independent spirit.

It was fantastic, running at that pace back then, and the feeling for both of us I think was that there were no hard edges; that there was space all around us.

We bought a carton of crickets and rented cane poles. We paddled out from the lodge to the edge of a weedbed and dropped a baited cricket down into the cooler, deeper waters at the edge of that fringed shelf, the edge of mystery.

It never took long. The bream were living back in that jungle of seaweed. They would dart out to grab the cricket, then dash back in with it. You had to be quick, had to keep a tight line, had to be fully focused and maximally alive.

They were huge for bream, to the point of being mythic. Every one of them was over a pound, and the largest were closer to two pounds. It was a nation of giants. We forgot about the bass fishing, the fancy rods and reels, the crankbaits and Mister Twister worms.

The lake—formed by damming the Sabine River for flood control—had filled so quickly that the trees it covered had not had time to die and topple over but remained upright, creating legendary fish habitat and, from an angler's perspective, a fantastic piece of luck in that the reservoir would never become a water skier's paradise due to the ghostly snags of the old East Texas forest that remains underwater to this day. Spars and snags lurk everywhere, so that narrow boat lanes are the best way to navigate the immense lake, with the low-slung bass boats trolling quietly just above the old forest, where the big bass live now like birds among the mossy branches.

You can't go back but sometimes you can't resist trying. And just as surely, there is a last time for everything. It's thirty-five years later, and when my father—who's just coming out from battling a couple of bad cancers, having spent years in the hospital—tells me he and his brother, my Uncle Jimmy (eighty, and a stroke survivor), are going back up there to fish again. I think, *Sounds great but I don't have time for this*. Then I think, *What really matters?*

You don't want to be morbid, but here's the deal: at some point, everything you do has to eventually be the last time you do it. Sometimes you don't know it's going to be the last time, other times you do, and still other times you don't know but have a pretty fair idea.

There is the distinct possibility that the cliché bumper stickers that proclaim the hours spent fishing are not taken away from one's allotted life are true—but what motivates me more to make this trip is the possibility that the opposite is true. That eventually there comes a last fishing trip. That even time spent fishing—the most leisurely and timeless pursuit of all—eventually runs out.

It's been a long time since the three of us fished together. It's been a long time since I was a boy of six or seven and they were showing me how to bait the hook. Hooking a fish for me and letting me reel it in. Taking me to the muddy stock tanks around Fort Worth—brilliant summer heat, grass as tall as I was, grasshoppers clacking up into the zodiac sun, giant cows lowing, frogs squeaking and leaping at water's edge—and casting out into those mysterious brown waters. A long time. I think we have all given a fair accounting. I guess it depends on how you measure things. Maybe the best unit of measurement of all is that nearing the end of your life your kid is willing—wants—to go fishing with you.

★

Uncle Jimmy's asleep when I get in. Dad's been waiting up for me, and it's great to see him after having been gone for a couple of months, and great to hear his plans and schemes for a fish. He was surprised by my last-second plane-ticket acquisition, and he seems surprised that I made it here in the dark, to this lost little cabin, utterly quiet apart from the shrill of insects, and unpeopled; we're the only guests.

"I could hide out here," he says. "I could come up here for a week, and just fish, and read."

The sun is up over the water by six, a copper-orange disk blazing through the pines and the cypress, infusing the day with the ascending power of hope, It's another glorious postcard sunrise, and though you've seen maybe thousands of them, they get you every time, reminding you that life is amazing and that anything can happen. Our guide, Stephen Johnson—a professional bass fisherman—coasts his boat quietly into the old weathered-wood slip at 6:25 a.m., introduces himself with a professional's good cheer. Hermit that I am, I can't imagine a harder job. Aren't there days where you don't feel like being friendly? If he ever has them, this isn't one.

He says the bream-hunting is pretty tough right now, but that he thinks we can find some crappie.

My father helps Uncle Jimmy into the boat. I stand close by, resisting the urge to help both of them into the boat. Part of me wants to shake my fist at this suddenly rapid disintegration of the body (it was *not* rapid; life is long—it only seems short, looking back), and yet part of me is so happy to be having one more fishing trip that I feel nothing but great fortune.

My father and uncle have been in the oil business since, it might seem, the oil business began. Maybe not that long, but that's how it seems. Dad is a geologist and has, over the last seven decades, found a lot of oil. Uncle Jimmy ran a company that fabricated steel pipe, mostly for oil-field purposes; over the last seven decades, he's threaded and sold a lot of pipe. Understatement, but none of it matters. It was all only but a moment.

And then, what makes the whole trip worth it, if nothing else happens—if we had to turn around and leave right now—is this: Captain Stephen getting out beyond the no-wake zone, out onto the big lake proper, and giving the boat full throttle, and us surging forward across the flat surface and into the cool, clean, lake-scented air with a feeling that is exactly, forgive the cliché, like flying.

The surge blows our hair back and the lake air washes past us. We inhale it deeply, and we find ourselves grinning like six-year-olds, as if having completely forgotten this feeling in which the physical act of soaring matches the imagined act of flying. The intersection between imagination and reality defines the territory where anything is possible, and where no infirmities exist.

It was once this way. That feeling has been gone so long that we have accepted—perhaps decades ago—the condition of rounded edges, or rounder edges, that replaced it. But here it is, totally unexpected, back, after having been gone for all those years.

We just grin and relax. Dad's three years of hospital bouts wash away, and Uncle Jimmy's speech and walking therapy wash away too. We're flying.

★

Stephen steers our boat into an unpeopled cove, dark water, and tosses a buoy over, taking only the quickest of glances at his depth and fish finder. I'll soon come to understand that he knows the underwater terrain of the old mysterious forested valley that lies beneath us the same way my father and uncle know the buried landscapes of the oil fields my father's discovered and the buried landscapes into which Uncle Jimmy's steel pipe has been set.

Wasting no time, he's handing us our rods, complete with sliding corks and baited minnows—he's brought fourteen dozen!—and we drop the weighted lines over, the bobbers measured to descend to the magical crappie-depth of twelve feet.

As he's handing us our poles, he's explaining the basics to us: how to wait for the bobber to go all the way under, and how, if the hook manages to get stuck on an underwater branch, to not jerk and yank, because that will spook all the other fish hiding in that brush.

I particularly like this image: a flock of crappie roosting in all the branches, exploding into flight at the tug by one impatient fisherman, crappie flashing in all directions like quail, and Stephen tells us it may take some getting used to learning to fish with a bobber again.

There is no room for anything but one thought, no room for anything but the waiting.

The wait isn't long. Suddenly Uncle Jimmy has a fish aloft, is swinging it into the boat, and it's a huge crappie—our goal, more precious than jewels or any other riches of the earth, gleaming in the morning light, every scale illuminated with fantastic clarity.

Uncle Jimmy is grinning like he rarely grins, the ear-to-ear kind, and even Stephen, who has seen so much, seems a little surprised by the immediacy of the success. He unhooks Uncle Jimmy's fish and holds it up for me to photograph, the two of them still grinning, and with Uncle Jimmy giving a thumbs-up.

Stephen re-baits Uncle Jimmy's hook with a splendid shining minnow, and moments later he's got another one, almost as big as the first. Stephen says that's often how it goes; that the other fish in a school seem to get excited when they see one of their own rush out and take the silver minnow and then disappear—ascending!—and that they rush out and attack the next minnow, or minnows; and sure enough, now Dad has one on his line.

My own bobber begins to twitch, sailing a short distance under mysterious power, then pausing; and after a while, when it has moved no more, I reel in to see the archetypal image of woe and futility, the shining bare hook.

Dad and I are both losing bait now, while Uncle Jimmy is still hauling in one crappie after another, though finally he too hits a cold spell; I imagine a vast school of bream moving in, with some underwater communication going on. After we've gone through maybe three dozen minnows, Stephen announces quietly that he thinks we'll move on to another spot.

He's got plenty of other spots. Like a farmer, he gathers and binds great twisted bundles of tree limbs, trunks, and branches, as if creating some public-art installation, then tows them out into the lake and tosses them overboard to create microsites of extreme habitat: secret places known only to him, and which he guards and protects carefully—his livelihood. I don't probe him too much on this, but I wonder if he tows them out there on moonless nights, like a pirate or a rum-runner. The practice is legal; it creates structure and habitat that would otherwise be lost as the lake ages, slouching toward senescence. And, like a farmer, Stephen practices rotation on his underwater fields of fish, never harvesting more than ten fish from any one pile, and giving each brush pile a good rest between such harvests.

It feels a little sissified—especially having the guide unhook the fish—but we get used to it pretty quickly.

At every brush pile there are fish. I'm surprised we don't catch any largemouth, but Stephen says the crappie are more aggressive and keep them driven out of the prime habitat. At one pile we begin catching little yellow bass, each of them about a pound, and they, too, go into the ice chest so we can find out what they taste like. They look like circus fish, yellow-bellied and blazing with the distinct stripes of striped or white bass, bold as zebras. Particularly fascinating to me is the way the lines stop near the ventral region and then begin again, slightly offset, rather than continuing uninterrupted, as if a printer had run out of ink and then repositioned the fish for the remainder of the stripes, but with that slight offset.

Who made the world? writes the poet Mary Oliver. *Who made the swan and the black bear?* I puzzle over what selective advantage there could be for such desynchrony but can't figure out anything satisfactorily intelligent. The day is growing hotter, and it just doesn't feel much like a day for hard thinking. Marveling, yes, but straining my brain, not so much. Maybe the stripes are just an ongoing, random experiment. Maybe the verdict on such offsets—compared to the unbroken lines on striped bass—is that it is still a work in progress.

Stephen shows us on the depth finder the deeper, cooler channels, the meandering path of where the old Sabine River once was, or, I suppose, still is; a dark river of mystery now, buried, but still moving sluggishly.

The limit for crappie on Toledo Bend is fifty, but Stephen says he asks his anglers to fish to only twenty-five. As if seventy-five fish in the ice chest is modest.

In the end, the crappie are so large that our ice chest is filled with only fifty. A hundred fillets. The decimal system. Our family scrapbooks have pictures of Dad and Uncle Jimmy from when they were ten, and when they were twenty. Photos of me when I was ten, twenty, thirty.

Such thoughts hold steady, out on the lake, like a baited hook dropped overboard, with a bobber. Out on the lake, you have a chance to think about such things without getting in a rush, or feeling that something's getting away from you.

★

It's true enough, time did not move while we were out on the lake; all day long, it sat still and deep, while we pulled one fish after another from out of those brush piles, as we had done on a similar hot summer day thirty-five years ago.

Still, even after we got out of the boat and my father helped Stephen clean the fish, and we took them up to the cabin to cook later that evening over mesquite coals in the red dusk with no one else around, only East Texas summer-evening insect roar and birdsong—even then it wasn't moving. It would soon—it would resume its fluid rush, replete with eddies and center currents, standing waves, haystacks, riffles. And it occurs to me that old age can be extraordinarily interesting, and not a thing to be feared, if only because how you choose to spend your dwindling time—those hours when the fishing stops—matters more, with the hours so increasingly valuable.

Maybe your whole life has felt timeless, and only now do you fully understand—on a lake, with family—how the hours are becoming so finite.

What paradox, then! For in making the right choices, in the face of those dwindling important hours, it—time, the valuable thing—recedes yet again, for a while.

We sat around the grill, visiting. The fish was delicious. A few fireflies began blinking as night came on., They flashed as if looking for something, drifting lazily through the deep forest, as if searching for a deep hidden channel that might lie farther below—the route of where a river once ran, and which, though now buried, still wanders, well below the surface, but still every bit as vital as it is mysterious.

INTO THE WOODS
WITH JAMES MCMURTRY
Hunting Wild Turkeys, Great Songs,
and Wide Open Spaces

WHEN I STEP OFF the twin-prop plane in Wichita Falls, Texas, and into the late-day heat of spring, wind blasting forty miles an hour, the first thing I hear is a loud and live rendition of "The Star-Spangled Banner" by what sounds like a marching band. Wichita Falls is home to Sheppard Air Force Base, one of the busiest airfields in the US Air Force. The band is practicing, is all—it's no special occasion—but then the Warthogs go screaming past, and James McMurtry drives up in his old Ranger pickup, his wild Jesus hair silhouetted by the westering sun, and I get it instantly. This isn't just something he sings about—the heartland, rural values, hard choices, wars, politics—it's his world, his milieu.

Known best perhaps for his hard-rocking, driving-beat, social-protest songs, McMurtry has prodigious talents that exist far beyond the one-trick-pony stance of the angry troubadour. It's hard to articulate what's unique about his songs, but you know them the instant you hear them, not unlike a broad chain of deep-voiced male Southern white independent songwriting folk-country rockers with great guitar licks, great voices, great minds: Johnny Cash, Kris Kristofferson, Steve Earle, Joe Ely. Gruff and gravelly in tone, energetic guitar, gold-standard lyrics—there isn't any fluff anywhere. My own personal McMurtry favorite is "Holiday," an extended ballad about the stresses and expectations upon modern families to uphold traditions, setting out on the road in inclement weather, determined to have a good time, a time of family unity. The story would be touching on that level alone, but with each new stanza, the stakes are raised.

He's a traveling musician these days—he has been for over twenty years—playing about 150 shows a year, with a weekly Wednesday night gig at the Continental Club in Austin. It's a tough go, even in the best of times; it's a tough go now. Sometimes he travels with his band (a drummer, bass player, and sound man/guitarist); other times he's solo. His work has been influenced by other Texas legends—Guy Clark, Lyle Lovett, and Willie Nelson—but his songs are unmistakably his own. Writer Stephen King says, "The simple fact is that James McMurtry may be the truest, fiercest songwriter of his generation."

In some things—his guitar work, for instance—he's precise: just so, almost cautious, striving for perfection. In other things—such as the interior of his old truck—he's a little less so. Priorities. Loose change sprawls on the floor and car seats. Split plastic cups crinkle underfoot, receipts flutter, empty plastic water bottles roll like bowling pins. He drinks a lot of water, probably between one and two gallons a day, as if trying to quench some burning inside.

His paternal great-grandfather moved to Archer County from Missouri in the 1880s; his grandfather said that at the turn of the twentieth century, there were "three mesquite trees" in the whole county. Then the mesquite swarmed over due to the white culture's overenthusiastic suppression of all wildfires. The mesquite destroyed rangeland by crowding out grasses, once a valuable thing. Then there was a big play for oil, but it's going away; the last of the oil is way deep. Now the mesquite is the valuable thing because it provides cover for deer and turkeys, which allows landowners to lease their land for hunting.

Landowners are locking up their land, folks he refers to as

"the high-fence guys," trying to keep deer on their land like live-stock, rather than wild animals that are free to come and go. He doesn't like it but he drives on, steady and easy. If you're wondering whether he's related to the writer Larry McMurtry, he is; Larry's his dad. I'm here to talk to James about music, not his father's writing, but I can't help but think of the title, *Horseman, Pass By*.

We're driving straight out to the Langford ranch, owned now by his dad and Aunt Judy and Aunt Sue, to scout for turkeys; to listen for them going to roost, so we'll know better where to set up and hunt in the morning. He doesn't rhapsodize over the land's beauty—the outrageousness of an arid land made so briefly green—but anyone can see that the land fulfills him. He points out the scissor-tail flycatchers swooping along the road and notes that when they show up, it means there won't be any more freezes. Likewise, the newly emergent leaves on the mesquite trees, the last to bud out.

I'm surprised by how much he talks about his grandfather Jeff, who evidently threw a pretty big shadow. Hell, his father, Larry, casts an immense shadow in Texas. I imagine it can't always have been easy, being James, Son of Larry, but he seems to have figured it out.

★

We park and wander the woods looking for tracks, or feathers, and listening for gobbling. There's nothing but a high howling wind. James points out a creek that gets real high once in a while. He says that in the old days there were a couple of times when the waters would rise so quickly and so high they would cut off the cattle from their main pasture. His dad would have to ride over and get them and push them back across, swimming. It was dangerous business, he says, because cow ponies in Archer County didn't have much practice swimming. A cowboy drowned, over on the North Fork.

"I always wondered why they didn't put a wire gate on the south fence, run the cows across the neighbor's pasture and onto the county road where there's a bridge over the creek. I've never tried to make cows cross a bridge, but I'll bet they'd follow a pickup with a broken sack of cottonseed cake on the tailgate."

He's just visiting, pointing out the intricacies of his home, but as writers are sometimes wont to do, I can't help but remember that statement and wonder if it's not a subconscious comment that speaks in some way to his life and his career: going his own way about fame, taking the long way around, avoiding the pitfalls that so often plague the progeny of big shadows.

He's reckless yet precise. When I open the first gate, he asks to be sure that I close it in such a way that the cows can't nose the clip open. He's careful, too, with his guns. He shows me his old turkey-killing gun, a Browning Auto-5 twelve-gauge with a thirty-inch full-choked barrel, and an L. C. Smith that he says I'm welcome to shoot, but I decline, too broke for a license. He says Larry got a whole box of guns from an estate sale that he bought for the books alone. The guns came as an afterthought. James is definitely more interested in guns, says he's not much of a reader; when he was a kid, he didn't read that many books, though he says he was always stumbling over them, that they were stacked high everywhere.

★

The ranch is in a strange place geographically; within the span of only a few hundred yards, you can travel from lush green Southern hardwood creek bottoms, rife with birdsong and a soft green light filtering down through a canopy of hackberry and elm, and into an entirely different landscape, a long elevated ridge of caprock and mesa, with balanced rocks, tilted slabs, and the leavings of flint points. James shows me one site he's found in a broad basin, an intensely open spot looking out over the prairie with the gravel packed firm from foot traffic. There are fragments of tepee rings here and there. The view is sublime, and it's comforting and soothing to think of a culture nurturing itself, replenishing itself, year after year and generation after generation, in this one spot, staring out at what essentially is an unchanged landscape.

Just a little farther on there is a tilted mesa, a small mountain-top, where James says he's never found any chips or other artifacts; perhaps the mountaintop wasn't a gathering or socializing place, but a site for questing and isolation. We turn and wander back down toward the hardwoods. James says that when he and his band are on the road, most of the band members "always have their noses in books," but he likes to drive and just look out at the countryside and think.

Our plan is to split up, to spread out and listen. James directs me to a tall camo-shrouded hunting tower from which I can see a great distance. I should be able to hear any turkeys gobbling right before they fly up to roost, and maybe even hear the distinctive thwapping of their powerful wings. We'll mark the spot, then come back just before dawn and seek to call them down off the roost and into shotgun range (twenty-five, maybe thirty yards).

James disappears into the brush, toward the distant sound of gobbling. It's incredibly windy up in the tower, and after a while I can't hear the gobbling. I don't know if the birds have hushed up or if they're moving—perhaps toward us, perhaps away. It's a pleasant place to just sit and rock. The branches swaddle the tower, making a hidden bower that creaks.

At dusk, a giant black boar comes trotting out of the thicket, coming from the exact place where James had entered the woods. He's a big fellow, with tusks like a vampire's fangs. I wait for what seems a long time but finally I see James's head lamp coming toward me in the darkness, and from the gait of his approach, he does not appear to be hurrying. I tell him about the boar and show him the picture on my camera—kind of a fine-arts film-noir-looking image, a blurry black, bear-shaped animal galloping through the dusk—and James allows it might be good to take his pistol with him into the woods in the morning.

We drive back to the ranch house. Heat lightning is flashing to the west. For dinner James cooks a couple of giant venison steaks he's been marinating all day, and we drink wine out of plastic yellow saucers from the pantry. There is very little furniture, but the shelves are all lined with books, top to bottom. If you are not a reader, there seems to be nothing to do here but play music or write. It's a place to rest and sleep between hunts: Spartan, spare, elegant, secure. It appears not to have changed in a long time.

When I comment on the beauty of the simple plank table, James says it's something Larry got in an auction. "Larry has an eye," he says. "I don't have an eye for aesthetics." And I don't think he's being facetious or self-deprecating, just honest. I think his talents are not so visual or cinematic, but story-based—ballads and voice. His girlfriend, Kellie, describes his songs as often being "about people who are bent but not broken." He gives these people the dignity of "picking them up and carrying them for a little while," she says. Often, too, the songs are about ghosts, and the going-away of things.

James says his grandfather built this house out in the country on the same site where the original house burned in 1928. The summer James was fifteen, he came back from Virginia and lived in town with his grandfather, who would wake him up early every morning. One morning James slept in and didn't awaken until an old friend of Jeff's came in and stirred him, saying only, "Well, Jeff's gone."

★

While James cooks—a lone yellow lightbulb hangs in the kitchen, the venison in a black iron skillet, olive oil marinade, cream gravy, fried potatoes simmering—I ask him how connected he feels to

Texas. His answer informs me that he considers Texas to be identified more by the land under his feet than the people who flow briefly across it.

"I love the hunting and fishing here, and the countryside, and my kin," he says. "But I don't consider myself as Texan as they are. I don't consider myself a Texas musician because my songs are as likely to be set in Maryland as they are in Texas."

As with a lot of great songwriters, his songs have been covered by surprisingly few others, and I think in large part it's because he so thoroughly owns the sound of the songs he writes and sings that it would be daunting, hard to imagine them being sung by anyone else, famous or otherwise.

It's tricky, he says, trying to figure out how to "assemble a career." He doesn't pass up jobs any more. On the drive in from Wichita Falls to Archer City, he pointed out a decrepit out-of-business honky-tonk where he played once. It can be a hard road to travel, he says, but he doesn't seem concerned. Instead, he seems relieved, seems happy to be going hunting in the morning.

His mother taught him his first guitar chords when he was seven. He went to boarding school but didn't care for it, went to college but didn't care for that so much either. He tended bar for a while, worked on movie sets, including Daisy Miller and Lonesome Dove—in the latter, he was the kid who wouldn't go in the whorehouse—and did a little nondescript cowboying on sets. But mostly, just music.

Awards and enumerations are no way to measure an artist, but he's recorded ten albums, including a 2005 single, "We Can't Make it Here," which won Best Song. The record it was on, Childish Things, won 2005 Best Album by the Americana Music Association.

★

Somehow it's gotten to be late. The wine is gone, and I nurse a dark rye beer. A call has come in from one of John Mellencamp's band members, and I eavesdrop unabashedly as the two musicians shoot the breeze, with the lightning still raging outside, sitting at the dark plank table just at the edge of that small throw of yellow light, with the other musician's disembodied voice coming in from out of the dry storm.

Their long, late-night earnest discussion over the minutiae of certain songs and sounds makes it seem to me that James is encamped in some laboratory far out in the country, where art burbles and gurgles, getting made, getting fabricated, getting dreamed, and seeking release into the world—always seeking release into the world. It wasn't Robert Earl Keen who spawned it, of course, any more than it was Buddy Holly or even Townes Van Zandt, or anyone else. It was something older and deeper, and even though it seems those Old Ones have almost all gone away, and that thing has gone away, it hasn't; it's still out there in the soil, still coming up like a vapor, I think, in places, or like a spirit. And I think that to find it, you sometimes have to sit very still, like a hunter, and very quietly, and wait for such things to rise again and again.

I go out to sit in the lone lawn chair on the front porch and listen to that dry howling wind and watch the phantasmagoric lightning storm just a few miles off, over in Archer City proper, perhaps, which is bringing no rain. After a while James comes out on the porch with his guitar and plays an exquisite little series of chords, just noodling around. It sounds like some incredible classic folk song I've never heard before, like something Leo Kottke might play but without that stylish pop of self-awareness that sometimes accompanies, or rides just behind, such mastery, and when I ask James what song that was, he says it was just chords. I don't want to jinx it or badger him or interrogate him by asking if it's a song he's working on, so we just sit quietly and watch the storm. I don't really know how music works at all. Maybe he was just fooling with chords the way you or I might tap our finger without even knowing we're doing it—putting those chords together with the unthinking idleness of a grocery list, perhaps, which will be gone the next day, never to return. But it was one of the most beautiful and elegant little melodies I ever heard. After a while the storm calms down and goes away.

★

There are a lot of joys in the world, but there is none quite like the one known to the turkey hunter who, upon walking through the dimmest of predawn light, hears the first nearby gobble of a wild turkey, and who knows that whether or not they find a bird that day, there is going to at least be action; that the quarry is indeed in the woods. It is an electric sound, and an electrifying one; it seizes the blood. A lot of hunters will begin running toward the sound, but James just keeps on walking, staying cool; inside, though, he is not cool. No one can hear that sound and remain cool—no one. At best, you go to a tight small place between abandon and fierce control, and you slide along that narrow gauge, watching and listening, with all the senses so inflamed that it seems a single spark, mixed with a single gust of wind, could ignite you; that the world is almost—almost—too fine to inhabit.

You also know dimly that the morning will not last forever, and that you will either find, or not find, the turkey, and that even if everything goes perfectly, and you engage the bird—and the forest—with maximum intensity, burning aglow, the engagement, and the morning, will end. But all that is later—the sun will come up, gold light strafing through the new-green buds and foliage, and with the woods all around you thundering with the raucousness of wild turkey gobblers converging upon you, coming in from all directions, seeking your call, fanning and strutting and clucking and yelping and scratching, coming ever closer, searching

for the thing they think they want, while you are hidden motionless and camouflaged and perfectly still in the brush, with your
desire burning every bit as incandescent as theirs.

There is a perfect beauty in the world, and the world belongs
to you. It is yours to take, though to do so you must acknowledge
who and what you are, and what your position is in the place of
things—a hunter, one who comes and takes, and then goes away
for a while. One who participates in the life and death of the wild.

★

We're tucked into the thorny brambles of dagger-clawed green-
brier. The morning is so cool the mosquitoes haven't found us yet.
The birds have been calling all around us, answering James's slate-
call yelps, but not moving—spurning us, is what it feels like, as if
knowing the difference instinctively between the authentic and
the inauthentic. But James plays hard to get, is quiet for a while,
and they begin to move in. One bird calls on our right, sounding
closer, and then another one calls from our left, closer still. Carefully, I ease back farther into the thorns, in case the shooting starts.
All a turkey has to see is the slightest movement and he'll be gone,
a silent ghost melting away; you'll never even know he was there.

More gobbling, thunderous now, approaches cautiously, about
eighty or ninety yards out. They are magnificent in that green-
gold morning light, their feathers rippling with sun-struck iridescence—green bronze gold purple—and their fiercely ugly heads
are a luminous blue, their wattles crimson with agitation. They
look cautious as hell, like desperadoes slipping out of town, but
they're coming our way quietly, clearly confused as to why they
can hear a hen yelping but can't see it. They're looking hard, right
at us, and if either of us blinks, we're screwed.

Every step brings them closer to meat. Sixty yards, fifty—they're
moving slower, and we're both holding our thoughts vacant and
still, creating a void for them to come into, careful not to set up an

invisible wall of resistance with our desire, our longing, for those next ten or twenty steps.

They hang up; they pause, disconcerted. Looking right at us, thirty-five or forty yards out, with only some brush and saplings between us and them. One of them makes the little troubled putt sound that usually precedes their turning around and leaving, but it's the one in front, and he doesn't entirely want to leave and give up his spot at the front of the line to his two compatriots just behind him.

They stare at us for what feels like hours: six highly evolved bright, wide eyes glaring wildly at four narrow-slit hunter eyes, our faces swathed in camo netting. The young gobbler at the back fans, displaying; the lead gobbler sees something he doesn't like and steps back. The middle gobbler steps up into his place, and takes one more step beyond that, stepping just within that thirty-yard perimeter and into the open, and James fires—I've got my ear covered, anticipating, waiting—and the turkey slams down onto the ground with a flapping of wings and then is still, and the other two turn and scoot away, the bright blue color of their heads fading quickly to a duller color as they send the blood down to their legs, for running.

It's a big bird, though a young one. James readies himself for a second shot but none is needed: a good, clean kill. He walks over to examine his gift—his earned and hard-gotten gift—in that morning light, and after a few moments, I walk over to admire it with him.

Walking out, toting the heavy bird on his back—walking quietly but with a bounce in our step—remembering what it was like, and trying to hold on to the morning for as long as it will or can be held, James points out a series of strong cattle pens made out of oil-field pipe and sucker rod. He says that about fifty years ago a buffalo came through this country, and somehow the cowboys caught him and held him in those pens. They looked up his brand, James says, but couldn't find registry of it anywhere in Texas, nor in Oklahoma or New Mexico. They finally tracked it down to a rancher in Kansas, who said the bull had run away months ago and had been traveling all that time, no doubt leaving in his wake a string of torn-up insubstantial barbed wire, broken necklaces all the way to Kansas. It was just that bull's bad luck to finally come through this place that had such a capable holding pen—following, perhaps, the old ghost trails of buffalo a hundred and thirty years gone, or longer—and a couple of days later, the Kansas rancher drove down and picked his buffalo up, then went back home.

If the bull hadn't come through the McMurtrys' ranch, he might have made it all the way to the Gulf. It almost sounds like a song, I think, and I start to say so; but today, at least, James isn't working, and so we just walk on, quietly, and I watch and enjoy the morning, with stories, dense and thick, all around us.

INTO THE WILD

THERE IS ABSOLUTELY NOBODY in the parking lot, nobody on the trail, despite it being a magnificent spring day: blue sky, mild morning sun, and dogwood blossoms floating ethereal beneath the big pines. I'm with my best friend from high school, Kirby—a Houston suburbanite these days—and his youngest son, Cade, age fifteen. An hour or so earlier, the lady at the ranger station's front desk of the Sam Houston National Forest in New Waverly had no recommendations for any trail to take, had herself never been in the Little Lake Creek Wilderness—3,855 acres without a road, a long and skinny piece of land, the shape and size of the world's most miniature Idaho—and seemed almost curious about why we would want to, as if, the word *wilderness* should serve as a precaution. Why not just ask her where we could find a good butt-whipping? We tried to get a rise out of her by asking about bears, but she just lifted her eyebrows and said, *Officially, no bears.*

Was there anyone around who could recommend a trail for us to take?

No. We would be on our own. Into the wild. The first only officially sanctioned wild in Texas, grouped in with four others that—are you ready for this?—Ronald Reagan signed into law at the behest of Representative Charlie Wilson and others.

Sweet.

★

We park and step onto the South Wilderness loop trail; five or ten paces later, a sign announces we are in the wilderness. Wilderness with a capital W, designated by the US Congress in 1984. There's saw palmetto everywhere, reminding me of childhood Easter pageants in East Texas, where these were the fronds laid in church hallways for white-robed actors to walk across, scuffing and rattling.

We're not seeing much deer sign at all—the forest is too old, wonderfully old; the dense canopy screens out much of the sun and the photosynthetic transfer of energy into low-lying forbs on which the deer could feed. But about half an hour into our walk, we cross a creek between two higher pieces of land—mild swells, not unlike the bump in a bull snake that has swallowed a rodent— and in this hardwood bottom, there is a game trail speckled with the hoofprints of two or three small deer.

There's still not much sign, but this is where you might wait and watch, and I think for sure that if I worked in one of Houston's glittering skyscrapers, evaluating the language of oil and gas leases or executing tax law, I would have to come to this spot frequently in the autumn with my rifle or bow-and-arrow and sit quietly and wait, and hope, or go stark raving mad, caught in the throes and limbo and bowels of a life cut off from the rank, wild surprises and stimulations of a life spent at least part of the time in the out-of-doors.

Phrases worth examining for a moment: *out-of-doors* and *wilderness*. Free from tameness; busting out. Lighting out for the territory. There was a time, maybe only a generation or two ago, when that was still how we thought of ourselves—as Texans.

Cade asks his dad how far he thinks we've walked. He's not uncomfortable—not yet—he's just not had a lot of practice walking so far in a place where he's never been before. We could be going anywhere, we could be going nowhere, and his senses are understandably, justifiably, tingling. The sign said *Wilderness*.

Texas doesn't have enough wilderness. It has hardly any at all. Even after all the chopping and dicing, all the subdividing and ranchetting, all the fencing and roadbuilding, there are tens, maybe hundreds of thousands of ranches in Texas that are larger than this one little wilderness. This is one of the only ones, the first and the last, and it was legislated over a quarter of a century ago.

A quarter of a century ago, I was riding home in my truck from mill meetings in northwest Montana with a pistol under my seat. Bullies would follow me a short distance—I lived forty miles from town—while I argued with loggers and millworkers that we needed more wilderness in Montana, and bigger wilderness; some more wild places where we would never build roads, never run saws. Big wild places for young people to be young in.

They wanted it all. I was public land. They could not have it all.

I have never seen a wilderness designated that people did not come to love. In my life, it is a necessary and wonderful element.

And the farther we inch forward as a species, out on this tenuous branch, the more I think many, maybe even most of us, need it.

High above us, a jet is passing, and whether coming or going, Jacksonville or Tokyo, Minneapolis or Johannesburg, I have no idea. If each of us, any of us, had but one more day, how would we spend it? Where would we spend it?

If we had seven more days, or ten, or even twenty, how would we spend them?

What if we had a thousand more, or two thousand? How, some of them, and where?

A sweet and disturbing familiarity begins to spread into my mind with the mesmerizing quality of rising water creeping, where present boundaries and borders blur and contract. I know this country. I've been here. Not *here* here; and yet, so very much *here*. This is the country I grew up in, played and explored in; the country in which I first learned to love—need—nature. My childhood home in the suburbs, like those of so many others, chewed into the edges of this land back in 1963. My God, how did so much time tumble past?

★

You do not just step off from going seventy-five miles per hour on I-45—or Transnational 69, as they're now trying to call it, the rolling howl of commerce for the frenzy of our hungers. You don't just jump out of the Suburban and step into the wilderness, ready to become in your first three steps a child of God. That's not a graft that will take. The sun itself, glinting and sliding down off the shiny leaves of the canopy above, must come to rest upon you with a certain accumulated weight.

I don't shake off the first bit of road husk until we take our first break, sitting on a big fallen log.

Thank goodness for fallen logs, unexhumed, unharvested, resting and rotting in just the right place.

I've become one of those people I used to think were rare: citizens so ancient that it could be said about them that they had lived to see so very much history; had seen humankind land on the moon, had lived through wars, had seen all kinds of presidents and periods of economic prosperity, as well as dramatic financial calamity. Had used a slide rule in school, carried a metal lunchbox. Typed my early books on a typewriter. Suddenly, there is no real end to the evidence in support of my ancientness, and the recognition of this fact is felt in an onrush that is as physical as it is emotional. The shape of the land, the texture of the sandy soil of the ridges as well as the firm-packed mud of the lowlands—the scent of the just-right mix of pine needles and deciduous leaves that coat the forest floor—the strange feelings of solitude and solace that I first encountered in the woods, and which I quickly came to realize were not only delicious, but necessary: instant refuge in and from a world I did not yet know or understand. An other, fuller world.

Beyond the inestimable value of what we call, in all earnestness, *ecosystem services*, for which we don't have to pay one thin dime but which we could never afford to build or otherwise create ourselves—the forests filtering the air, the coral filtering the great oceans, the rivers and fires and floods and winds that keep the great garden stirred and moving, stirred and growing, in a just-right accounting of the living and the dying. Here in the woods, the world's greatest economy is still functioning, and when one is in its midst, one feels awed, grateful, finite, miniscule. One feels the humility of one's proportion. To me, this seems extraordinarily healthy.

We lost that, at some point; it disappeared. And yet somehow, and almost blindly, we still proceed. We are still here, a ravenous experiment, but the ground that made us is no longer here. Something else has taken its place—an unearned assurance; an undeserved arrogance.

Blackwater ponds, Spanish moss, crawfish scuttling in clear-water sand creeks, and the filigree of raccoon tracks: this is the country that made me believe in the wilderness, back when I was a child.

Kirby is looking all around, and up at the tops of trees, with the wonderment of a wallaby that has never touched the forest floor before. A small woodpecker, probably a red-bellied (*Melanerpes carolinus*), is drumming in the forest below the trail, and it is Kirby who notices the sound; to me it's just background noise. I'm still listless in my busy brain, remembering the Forest Service lady who advised us to not go into this nasty old wilderness. I'm still remembering the traffic, remembering billboards, remembering airline schedules, fretting about money. You can't go from zero to sixty in these matters.

Kirby leaves the trail as if in a trance, summoned by the drumming; I follow. We crane our heads but can't find the bird, though the drumming continues. I'm wandering around, fruitlessly, when

Kirby motions me over; he's found the correct tree by placing his hand on it and feeling the vibrations radiate down the trunk. He places his head against it and smiles as if receiving some kind of deep medication.

We travel on. A skink patters through the dry leaves. Kirby crouches, tries to catch it, but it's gone, though we dig through the duff looking for it. I didn't see it at all, and now I want to, with surprising intensity.

The trail winds, bends, curves. Something ancient feeds into us as our feet transcribe the shape of the land beneath us into our brains. Kirby stops, with the fascination of a child, at one of the little clear creeks that lace the woods with shimmering glitter. I've already leaped across, intent only on gaining the other side, but Kirby has paused on a tiny sandbar, pressing down on it with his foot, watching a trickle of bubbles come up at the far end of the spit. Bubbles of all sizes and shapes rise from below, as if some miniature spring resides there, and he stands there looking at it a long time, while all around us, the leaves unfold wider and ever greener.

The day is warming. Kirby is perspiring. At every rest stop, he and Cade drink water; my four airplane sample bottles are drained quickly, long before we reach the halfway point of the loop. I feel badly about this waterlessness—isn't the humidity enough?—and I wish I could do some kind of Bible trick, some sweet magic, to conjure unending sweet cool water for both of them.

The loop bends out of the wilderness, travels through some nicely managed big pines—Kirby spies another skink, and again, I miss it—and we pass now through a stretch of cutover woods. Some big pines remain, but there are stumps too, and weeds, and direct sun, and—is this possible?—a house, a regular old thing with a chimney and a driveway and kitchen windows and a basketball hoop.

Cade and Kirby, tired and thirsty, look long and hard at the house; I gaze into the woods below us. Our map shows we're at the corner of private and public property. There is a county road just below this square of private land, and the map shows we could walk over to that driveway, follow it out to a farm-to-market road, then to a secondary road, and hitchhike our way back to the other side of the wilderness. No one says anything. I will do whatever they want; they will do whatever I want.

I urge us down the trail. Cade looks back at the house with undisguised longing, and Kirby, ever an adventurer, hesitates. I feel as cruel as if driving a pair of rented mules with a whip, but we continue into the deeper forest.

Kirby spies another skink, yet again unseen by me. Damn.

We crest a ravine and see a goshawk leap from a branch. From our heightened advantage, we look down on it, as the goshawk itself must look down on voles, rabbits, small birds, mice. A swamp world, seething with bounty, just beyond the reach of the long arm of Houston, with the wisdom of a Congress that invested in this place for ever and ever.

We stop to rest again. Something's wrong with Kirby. His eyes are glassy and he's sweating like crazy, even when he sits on a log in the breeze. I sit next to him and show him on the map how we're about halfway; how the place where that hawk got up below us is where we've just about rounded the horn. The same distance yet to go, but with the trail still new, untraveled, unseen.

I don't know it yet, but Kirby is at that point where, medically, reason and good decision-making begin to flicker like the head lamps of an old Ford as it shudders down a washboard backcountry road. All I see is him studying the map and appearing to give it good and considered thought.

We could short-cut, I tell Kirby and Cade, leave the trail and go through the middle of the wilderness, but it'll be mucky. It looks short and easy on the map, but once you're in, it gets big quick. I've done this kind of thing a million times, and if we go in, I tell them, we're going to get lost—deliciously, gloriously, ass-kickingly so. Not until it's all over—late, late tonight, or tomorrow, or whenever we get out—will we be glad we did it. "I want y'all to hear me," I tell them. "If we do this, we will wish we hadn't." I love the anguish and confusion of being lost; I'd rather claw and scrabble and stagger and stumble than go back, beaten, over trail I've already covered. But most folks don't.

Cade is listening; he hears me clearly and does not like what I am saying. But Kirby is not hearing, or is hearing something else. His eyes are so glassy. He looks like he's listening to something far away, like when he was trying to find the drumming woodpecker.

"Let's go," he says.

For a little while, the going is easy. The light is softening; the sun seems heavier. We crest a long rise, wading through cutover young pines that are waist high. We clutch our map—on it, a few tiny veins, pale blue as an old woman's, course toward the center of Little Creek , and the plan we have is to find one of these threads, follow it perpendicular to the main creek, cross the creek, and then find the trail we started out on.

We walk slowly, not like the high school kids we once were, but like old gentlemen somehow lost. As if searching for the rest-home we have fled.

The forest is still beautiful—the same dogwood blossoms hang like floating snowflakes—but we are lost. We don't know what the path home will look like, but I cling to the idea that we will know it when we see it. Kirby is still sprouting water, and he keeps stopping after only a few steps.

He looks like he doesn't know where he is or what he's doing out here, which is, of course, a whole other scale of lost. I don't know what to do. From time to time I look at Cade, who looks so young, and I wonder how impossibly ancient his father and I must seem to him. I figure Kirby must just be having a bad day—tired from work, out of shape.

I walk as slowly as I can, but still Kirby lags, and whenever I look back, more often than not he is leaning against a tree or clutching his quads. When he sees my look of concern, he smiles, straightens up, and pushes forward, as if embarrassed for my having witnessed his discomfort.

We enter the thick forest; we find a creek, an artery of living water. It's reddish-black, algae-rimmed but seething with life: minnows and water striders. Kirby looks at it but does not drink. The creek meanders in a beguiling series of S's, and we creep and wobble through the forest's rotting, leaf-black bottom. We find an old flood-swept whiskey bottle and open it—there's a quarter-inch of amber in the bottom, smelling the same as it ever did—and Kirby, with a flash of mirth, swallows it.

How bad can he be, really? Still, he's walking so incredibly slowly, and stumbling, just as I said we would. He plows through the great arbors of poison ivy, tumbles down sand embankments and into the creek, the damp banks of which are limned with coyote prints and deer tracks: a veritable highway through the wilderness, six feet below the forest floor. The underground railroad.

The sun drops lower. At one point Kirby leans his full weight against what is surely the world-champion holly tree, its girth thick enough to mill for lumber. We pass on, come to a swamp, into which the tannin-bronze vein of the creek disappears; we have no more guidance. We make our best guess and press forward, and, on the other side of the swamp, find it again.

The light has gone to olden tintype, coppery and blood-infused, making it seem as if we're somehow auguring back into time. It feels like on the map we're making about fifty feet an hour, or as if we're drilling down through stone rather than gliding through the here and now. I find myself remembering that hawk; how, when we saw it fly away, it dislodged some ripe dogwood blossoms so that they fell, drifting in the heat, like snow. If this is to be a last day, it has been a good one.

Sometimes our way in the creek is blocked by a fallen tree so we have to climb out of the deep channel, back up to the forest floor and follow a game trail, stumbling again through thorns and poison ivy, with its Adam and Eve, fig-like leaves. At one such portage, Kirby can go no farther. He does not fall but kneels like a football player on the sidelines and stares into the forest.

Then he lies down.

"My heart hurts," he says. "My quads are cramping." He clutches his legs. Then he closes his eyes and either goes to sleep or enters a coma. His breathing is loud and chuffy and shallow, like that of an injured horse.

Cade—bad Cade, so accustomed to bedeviling, and being bedeviled by, his father, with whom he often gets into hijinks—doesn't know this is atrial fibrillation, and neither do I; instead, Cade circles his recumbent father with his camera, snapping away. Facebook fodder; the prone paterfamilias like a giant tree felled.

Kirby naps. The daguerreotype light makes him look like some mortally wounded Civil War soldier. Is he napping or is he dying? Cade and I continue to think he is merely out of shape, just more so than I would have guessed a person his age could be.

He has finally stopped sweating so profusely—is not sweating at all—but that may be because we long ago ran out of water. Cade and I sit next to him like hounds and shoo the mosquitoes away and watch him, willing him to get better. Waiting.

After about half an hour—blue twilight now—Kirby rises, unsteadily, and we resume our long creep through the darkened forest. We reach Little Creek in true darkness, splash across it, scramble through brush and up a steep slope, guessing and hoping, until almost miraculously we intersect the trail that the map assured us would be there—the same trail we strode on earlier in the day, with so much power and vigor and confidence.

We hobble an hour back to the car, where Cade has a tiny bit of Dr Pepper left, nothing else. A heated half-sip.

We drive to town, delirious.

And leaving the grocery store—carrying out armloads of vitamin water and bananas—we try to tell various people where we've been, but no one has heard of the wilderness, nor even the large national forest in which it is located, half an hour up the road.

We get rooms for the night in the town nearby. One of those extended exurbs of Houston. The long arm, the ever-extending tentacle. Malls, each one a battlefield of the soul, and hard for us to even look at after swimming amid the dogwood blossoms. Hydrated, Kirby is starting to feel better. We sleep again, dreaming swamp dreams.

In the morning, Kirby knocks on my door. He says his doctor had him on some new blood pressure medicine and he only this morning read the instructions for it. The label warned to avoid getting hot, and to avoid exertion, which could result in abnormal sweating and heart arrhythmia, followed by death.

It's more than sobering, and we marvel at our fortune; at how, by all rights, we should have gotten in far more trouble than we did. We marvel at how instead we had so much grace bestowed upon our little passage, our little hike.

What must it have been like, I wonder, when all the land was once this way?

We eat breakfast at some nondescript waffle place, not saying much, just remembering the day before, and listening, through the plate glass of the restaurant, to the roar of traffic out on the highway. Then we go outside, into the rising heat, and get in our car, and join the great hurried flow, heading back into the city, farther away from where we have been, briefly.

WRITING IN STONE

JOHN GRAVES HAS SLOWLY BUILT a reputation as one of the best writers in Texas. It's time the rest of the world caught on.

We've come not quite fully against his wishes. Our primary goal is to celebrate his ninetieth birthday, but a close second goal is to avoid overwhelming him with the praise that flows so easily from those of us who revere him, the best-loved writer in Texas and one of the least known beyond the state lines.

It's not that he's delicate, but he really just doesn't like to be around people. We've come a long way to find him, way out in the hill country southwest of Fort Worth. About a hundred of us have convened in a land where dinosaur tracks stipple the limestone riverbeds that wander through this scraggly—some would say desolate—heat-shimmering hilly land of juniper and sky.

I haven't seen John and his wife, Jane, in a few years, and this time when I darken the doorway at their ranch outside of the small town of Glen Rose, the elegant and beautiful Jane—formerly a designer back when she was Jane Cole—greets me with a hug and the query, "Do you remember that awful time you interviewed John at the Texas Book Festival, in the rotunda at the state capitol? The two least talkative people in the world, expected to have a conversation!"

A thousand or more spectators had been out there in their plush seats, eagerly watching the hermit of Glen Rose, awaiting whatever sage comments the clever questioner—I—could elicit from him.

Jane is happy to see me, but something has brought this unfortunate memory back to the surface. She jogs my memory and repeats, in case I've forgotten it, my first question to him: "So, John, you live in the country?"

The audience—who had read everything he's written, most of which has concerned his life in rural Texas—waited. After some deliberation, John said, "Yes," and then we both turned to look at the clock on the wall.

Obviously, Jane is still mischievous, though I also worry that it's not all teasing. It was ten years ago! They both have high standards in people, in art, in the written word. Jane is still an active reader, plowing through a great depth and breadth of literature each week, year after year. I think that for each of them there is some kind of invisible and unable-to-be-articulated code of being, a kind of ethos of personal craft that feels olden and in some peculiar way densely Texan.

★

The party is being held out beyond John and Jane's remote four hundred acres, named Hard Scrabble, where they live in a stone house that John built himself back in the 1950s. Their home is spare, appointed with a few select antiques, but the ranch where the party is being held is anything but spare. It, too, is hidden back in the juniper hills outside of Glen Rose, but it's a palace of Texas opulence—not a little stone house, but a mansion. Children swim in the large pool beneath glittering stars, and the testimonials circulate all night. The day was brutally hot, but tonight there is a dry breeze stirring, sliding down over the limestone cliffs and drying-out creek beds. There's a sweetness of introductions, in the bewitching dusk—everyone who knows one another is introducing their friends to those of us who do not, as if, drawn by the power of Old John, we seek somehow to unify before darkness falls. A hundred is not too many.

John is dressed dapper, looking like a swell, a venerable golfer, in a pink short-sleeve shirt and khakis. His silver-white hair, still plentiful, glows, and he has what used to be called a healthy tan. He sits at a table like the lion he is in Texas, his thick horn-rimmed glasses so old they have come back in style. He receives the unending flow of well-wishers, smiling his slightly embarrassed, lopsided looking-away grin, surely counting the hours and minutes until this ridiculousness ends. Indulging us.

There are not so many days and years left for him as there used to be, to say the least, and here he is spending one of those days on this kind of foolishness. The price of being rich with friends. Friends from the oil field, family from all around the country, his editor at the University of Texas Press, Shannon Davies. Bill Wittliff, a dear family friend, screenwriter for Larry McMurtry's *Lonesome Dove* and Jim Harrison's *Legends of the Fall*. Fellow *Texas Monthly* writers, including Stephen Harrigan and Elizabeth Crook. Folks from all over Texas, and all over the country.

When I spy an opening and accidentally cut in front of his fellow Marine, the screenwriter Bill Broyles, I tell John that it's good to see him and ask if he'd rather be somewhere else, anywhere else.

"Yes," he growls gently, smiling. "I would."

The party presses, crushes, rushes past, flows around him. It's a wonderful evening, enchanted, and we all move through it as if bobbing in a current. The pace of the river has gotten interesting, has quickened, while at the same time splaying into various criss-crossing braids. This is what rivers do naturally when they're not dammed. His relationships have characteristically been so isolated and focused that many of us don't know him in the context of anyone other than one or two others, and we stay late into the night, eating, drinking, listening to music, and unifying.

John himself retires to bed early. He doesn't hear any of the tributes, thank God. They're all wonderful; it just would have been painful for him. The one that brings the house down is from a young filmmaker, Rob Tranchin, who showed up at John and Jane's ranch one day, determined to solicit John's help in making a documentary about the legendary Texas naturalist Roy Bedichek. Rob essentially laid siege to John, camping on Hard Scrabble until John relented and said "All right."

Rob sent John a copy of the documentary when it was done, waited a while, then couldn't wait any longer. He called him up to see what he thought. He apologized for roping John into something he really didn't want to do, said he felt bad about it.

"There was a long silence on the phone," Rob says. Finally John spoke. It was a pretty good John Graves sentence: long in the making, and utterly considered. "You know, Rob," he said, "guilt can be an instructive emotion."

★

The CliffsNotes version, distasteful to a true fan or acolyte—for how do you fit ninety years into a few sentences?—must nonetheless be presented. He was born in 1920 in Fort Worth. Despite the drift of his childhood friends to the University of Texas in Austin, he attended Rice. It's an old story: An intelligent young person meets professors who change his life. Despite the ravenous bookishness of his studies and his formidable intellect, he's never been snooty—like many Texans, he has leaned perhaps overmuch in the other direction. This may be one of but many reasons Texans love him so much. He has not just maintained his rural roots but has tended them and preserved them with integrity—has embraced the rough edges that many Texans find so hard to sand down.

As young people must—obeying the territorial imperative— he sought to escape. He joined the Marines, became a captain during World War II, saw several battles, then was wounded by a grenade, which cost him his vision in his left eye and embedded other shrapnel he still carries. He ended up being in the hospital during the battle of Iwo Jima.

After the war, he went back home, then to Mexico, had high adventures, then veered north to Columbia University, read and wrote and studied with Martha Foley, Joseph Wood Krutch, Mark Van Doren, Lionel Trilling. His first published short story was in *The New Yorker*. Back to Texas, then to Spain, where he lived for a few delicious years, spent some time in France, read, and wrote.

Then his dad got sick. The pull of landscape and family brought him back, and, as if his orbit had been too wide, he returned to earth. He cared for his dad, stayed in Texas, never left again. He married Jane, bought a farm in the rough limestone hill country, named the ranch Hard Scrabble, and entered more deeply that strange nexus that no one, least of all the protagonist, can ever identify as chance or destiny.

Goodbye to a River is the work that made his in-state fame. The book—published over sixty years ago, a nonfiction account of Graves's three-week-long solo canoe trip down part of the Brazos River that had just been condemned to be buried beneath the slack waters of a series of dams built largely for recreational purposes, between the fetchingly named Possum Kingdom Reservoir and Lake Whitney—is a clear-eyed elegy for a natural history, and a wildness, that was slipping away even before the dams were proposed. *Goodbye* was one of the first "down the river" narratives, and it ran the narrow seam with typical Gravesian honesty between lamentation and celebration, dwelling in neither hope nor despair, only each day's beauty.

A few other books followed, ever so slowly. He was busy keeping bees, building stone walls and stone houses, tending stock, and reading, always reading; and writing, sometimes, though very carefully, painstakingly. He kept tinkering with a novel he'd begun as a young man in Spain. Then a long dry spell: lots of stone work. Two rocks on one, one rock on two; building things that would last. The days of middle age, out in the pasture on his farm, doing the things that men have done for thousands of years.

This is where his life gets most interesting—to me, at least. John describes those years as such:

> My old fascination with land and creatures and natural forces woke up with a vengeance, leading me into the building of a house and barn and corrals and fences, the supervision of herds of cows and goats, and the dozens of other activities that functional rural life entails.
>
> I had the grace to feel a little guilty about all this from time to time, for a puritanical part of my psyche has always regarded time spent away from books and writing as time wasted.
>
> Which has not, however, kept me from wasting lots of it . . .

It's an existential question: books, or the living? You can't take books with you when you go. For that matter neither can you take your days spent working on the rock walls and farm, but somehow, to me, those days seem more . . . *real*. Rarer, somehow, than books. You can write when you're old. You can't live as physical a life when you're old. The whole process—a life of quality, meaning, and balance—seems in some ways a question of timing.

What I love about John and his life is this: It's taken him ninety years, but he's done both. He built the rock walls of his home and got some books written. Ninety years have passed, and thirteen books have emerged; not like volcanoes, but in a slow igneous seep that has nonetheless managed, across time, to cover an entire landscape, and to harden. New generations of readers have wandered across the now-venerated literary landscape.

All but one of the dams proposed for the Brazos were turned back, in large part due to the craft and quality of Graves's description of a beautiful and meaningful thing that had been squandered. The beauty of his work endures, and there is a greater pride in Texans' hearts for our home, I think, than there would be if he hadn't written the books he did.

★

In some ways, what John means to me is extraordinarily simple—a writer is afforded, if one is lucky, only a handful of true literary heroes, mentors in both word and the examples of their lives, in a profession fraught with occupational hazards—though in other ways what he means to me is extremely complicated, particularly when I consider the dangerous no-man's-land between art and activism. He had a spell of do-goodism, working in DC briefly during the Johnson administration, and contributing to a book on water policy with the Sierra Club. He also had more than his share of war, but he moved strongly and quickly away from the debilitating toxins of both of those things and wrote about the land, and people on the land—individual lives.

Part of this willful separation between art and activism has to do with his famous intellectual honesty. In the classic *Self-Portrait, With Birds*, he laments in beautiful prose the passing of plover that used to migrate by the millions but reminds himself and us that what he damns mostly is having never seen them in such numbers. "But God, to have viewed it entire, the soul and guts of what we had and gone forever now, except in books and such poignant remnants as small swift birds that journey to and from the distant Argentine and call at night in the sky."

Like a mason whose task is both beauty and functionality, beginning with every stone chosen, the writer must first serve the text itself, not some ulterior goal. You can't get in a hurry with stonework. The stones are heavy, and the cumulative weight of the lifting involved must be spread across time; you can't lift a ton with a single heft, a single hoist. The stonemason's work is the architecture of patience and the architecture of love: love of the way the world works, and a silent howl of protest against the way it sometimes does not work.

It's complicated. I love how he never wrote a book for any reason other than that each was the one book he most wanted to write. How he eschewed the pursuit of a career or political correctness, choosing art, first and only. One of his latest books is called *My Dogs and Guns*, for Chrissakes—an inventory of weaponry he's owned, and notable circumstances of the guns' provenance, and memorable firings.

Paradoxically, he doesn't hunt. Even as a young man, he never cared for killing deer.

★

The next day, early on the morning after the big party, some of us go out to his ranch to hang out more, hungry for more of his company. All John wants to do in his ninety-first year is what he has always done: live on his farm, get up and work in the morning, tinker with things a little, then read, and go to bed, only to get up the next day and do it again. When his two daughters were growing up and decided, despite their affection for Hard Scrabble, to go to school in "town" (Fort Worth), Jane rented an apartment there, while John spent as much time as possible at home in the country, back and forth in the seam between work and family, and between the land and family.

Immediately after breakfast, he makes his break from the social setting of well-wishing that has invaded his routine and bolts straight for his office, a stone room with a screen porch. The office—filled with books, of course, floor to ceiling—is, like most of his house, not air-conditioned. The only concession he's made to the heat is to have a little fan blowing the outside air in through the open door, stirring the neat papers on his desk slightly. On this one day, only this one day, instead of writing, choosing and arranging words, he gives the day up to us and receives visitors yet again as we filter in, all morning long, to sit with him in his stone office and look around and catch up on things, and to tell him what he and his work have meant to us.

There cannot be that much time left now—all men are mortal; we know it and yet we forget or ignore it, each of us, almost every day—but for us, he will give up one of those days, and suffer the rain of our ceaseless praise.

We take turns going into his hallowed office to sit with him. When my opportunity arises, I summon an old dilemma, one I've discussed with him many times before, and which he, perhaps better than anyone, can understand.

"I still don't have it figured out," I tell him. It feels ridiculous, at fifty-two—middle-aged, yet roughly half his age—to still be groping: literature, or family? Books, or life? The glory of making a stone wall is so incredibly satisfying—incomparable, really, every bit as good as making a nice story or an essay or even finishing a book. The epigraph to John's 2005 memoir, *Myself and Strangers*, is a quote from Juan Ramón Jiménez's *Maximus: "Busquemos la gran alegría del haber hecho"* ("Let us seek the great happiness of having done").

There are certain times when his grenade-struck left eye fixes on you, through random drift, and you swear he can see with it, and better and deeper than back when it was sighted. Here in his office, visiting about what matters, this is one of those times. He says nothing about my dilemma—as if to say *it's your path, not mine, you have to figure it out yourself*—but he smiles, watching me edge closer to the place I try to resist, that books *do* matter, much as we sometimes would like to tell ourselves they are but a hobby.

He points to a row of old books on a lower shelf: gifts from a passing-through Frenchman who'd been towing a trailer full of expensive horses and had broken down near Glen Rose, maybe fifty years ago. The traveler had spent the day conversing with

John about art and literature while they worked on the trailer, then sent John the books as a thank-you gift. It was the perfect day, he might be telling me, with his anecdote: the perfect mix of art and labor. The sun beating down in August. A little welding torch, a lot of impatient horse whinnying, a lot of impassioned talk as they worked, and a little wine later that night.

The days that make a life. Do not be afraid to turn away from books, I think he is saying, remember to live life, even as he is pointing me to them, asking, *Have you read this? Have you read that? Did you ever read so-and-so?*

Do your best, he is telling me, do what you have to do. Literature is your master; serve it, but try to be a free man, too. Go back and forth between the two worlds. Eventually—always—one of them will claim you. But there is great virtue in the trying—the passing back and forth.

From such conflict and struggles, the soul is forged.

★

I suppose what I want to say about the largely invisible John Graves is that even a man of such unrelenting dedication to his craft, and to the rhythmic routines of life in the country, can be a bit of a paradox: too much unknown to general readers, and yet hugely celebrated by some, and, most important, by those who matter most.

It is not an insignificant thing to me to know that a man can live out in the country for most of his life, can marry a beautiful and elegant woman and live happily thereafter, and that they can raise two daughters who, perhaps in part because of, or perhaps in part in spite of, a deeply rural upbringing, turned out perfectly fine, more than fine. And make books the way he wants to, and to make a living at it, even if just barely sometimes, through thick and thin, across the decades, across major parts of two centuries. His might even be the kind of life people would envy, if only they knew about him.

3,822 MILES

I'M ONLY FOURTH GENERATION. Not old enough to remember buffalo, but old enough to remember my grandmother, who heard her father tell about them. My daughters would have been fifth generation, and then their children, perhaps sixth, but I went and fell in love with a place, Montana, that is in some respects now like what Texas was like, in the way-back: unbounded.

Wait, that's bullcrap. Texas has always been bounded. For as long as there have been rivers, there have been boundaries. Sometimes the people who lived here before paid attention to them; other times, not. The rivers were just rivers, not fences.

What I mean to say is I fell in love with a place, Montana, which, like Texas once upon a time, *imagines* it has no boundaries. A place where you can set out walking and never stop. A place so big that time sometimes seems to collapse, crumple, vanish.

Time never vanishes. Time is a river cutting always at everything. In our most blissful moments, we do not see this, or we are unaware of it.

From the air, however, you can see it in an instant: time on the move, and on the prowl. One of the words often associated with *beauty* is *timeless*, and in the magnificent images by fifth-generation Texan Jay Sauceda, the compositions of which portray with great elegance the colossal force of change, there is nonetheless beauty. He catches the two forces—change/erosion/conflict, as well as beauty—in a way that is both frightening and invigorating.

Many of Jay's images have to them the feel of beauty glimpsed just this side of some sort of apocalypse. *Our apocalypse*, I guess you'd call it. And if time is a river, maybe beauty is a river as well: striving to insinuate itself, with the fluidity of a river, in between the sharp edges of diminishment and change.

As T. R. Fehrenbach noted in his classic, *Lone Star*, Texas has had a longer continuous run of war along its borders than any other country in modern history. And today another world war involves all nations, as sea levels rise, crops scorch, groundwater depletes, fracking fluids contaminate, the ozone layer thins, and borders dry out, wither, and crack. Dust sweeps across old invisible dashed lines.

I want to reiterate, then: what I love about Jay's photos is that while they possess a curative beauty, it is not saccharine or unearned. His photos capture the slow terror of overpopulation and resource consumption that exists, like an arrow fired, in the heart of beauty.

They capture also the dignity of solitude that still remains—miraculously—in vast stretches of West Texas where—almost a blessing—there is no water, and hence no river of people.

But that's just my own quasi-misanthropic view. What's evident also in these photos is Jay's democratic and encompassing love for all of the state—the peopled and the unpeopled—and his naturalist's eye for the beautiful, wherever it might have gone to ground, gone to roost. He finds it—seeks it out—wherever it lies, wherever it is; and he proves here that it, like life itself, has a will to cohere, a will to endure.

The landscape of Texas has endured much in the past generations. Less is left than before, and there is much about the future that is—that word again—*frightening*. Jay's work is a major narrative in the history of the literature of one of the Union's most important states, under any criteria: a work as significant and powerful as John Graves' *Goodbye to a River*, Robert Caro's *Path to Power*, Edna Ferber's *Giant*, or, again, Fehrenbach's *Lone Star*.

★

One of the many great things about flying the entire perimeter of Texas is that from the sky, you can see geology in motion. You can see, too, biology in motion—the amoeba-sprawl of us, the beehive unification of our basic needs: food, shelter, water. We can see the homes and the agriculture, and water's etchings, water's narrative.

The sky reveals the movement of time more surely than the snow reveals to a hunter the tracks of one's quarry. Look, you can see it, rushing past, hurtling past, even as we construct our arbitrary borders and boundaries designed to control and manage time. Three hundred and sixty five days a year, ten years per decade, ten decades in a century: what could be more abstract than the boundaries we seek to place on time? We fling numbers at the sky while below us the land gallops past. The very stone on which we stand is washing away, the ocean is around our ankles already, and still we hang our calendars on the refrigerator and pretend that time is plodding, or even, in certain hours, motionless.

How drastically our understanding of the story changes with even a modest gain in altitude, and how our perception of time changes as well. At that slightly greater elevation, we can see it moving, can see it for the living thing it is; and can see, too, how powerful it is. How unstoppable.

We negotiate for valuable minutes—the rarest thing, the thing that runs through our hands like water. Look at the dry country: water carved it, once upon a time, and still does; canyons are feathered with water's etchings, time evident like the fringed gills of a fish, gasping in the dry air, just as the land below us waits for rain.

You can start anywhere in this narrative, clockwise or counterclockwise. Jay started in Galveston, not so long ago the largest port in America—bigger than New York just an eyeblink ago, really—and then he flew around the perimeter of the state, low and slow, snapping photos the entire way.

In Montana, where I live now—where water is scarce—the borders often consist of the knife edges of mountains, ice-shaved, sharp as obsidian. A bird—an eagle—glides freely from one state to the next, its morning shadow still in Idaho even as it crosses into Montana.

Here in Texas, however—whether in the lush forested country of East Texas, or the drier red country north, or the thorny lands to the south—the elusiveness of water defines our borders, real or imagined. Is it for this reason, more than any other, that there has been so much war, and for so long? That water, unlike stone, refuses to be owned?

The Sabine, the Red, the Rio Grande, the Colorado, the Canadian: the state's heart is made of rock and soil, but we are contained by water, which must be shared with the sky, shared with the soil, shared with everything.

★

There are a lot of us. There are so many more of us than there were before. What are our dreams now? How have they changed?

Beneath our feet, does the soil, does the state, still urge us in certain directions, influencing our dreams? Does it still whisper to us, if ever it did (and I believe it did)? If it does, can we still hear it?

Looking at what I think of as Jay's water photos from the east side of the state, I find myself remembering my childhood rainy days in Houston spent listening hopefully to the lightning-static crackle of AM radio weather reports calling out hurricane coordinates—Carla, Beulah, Cindy. I remember the eerie beauty of green skies, skies the color of various bruises, birds flying low and fast. I remember hoping, hoping, I would not have to go to school that day. Plotting the slow and curious drift, the coordinates, with tiny magnets, coordinates on the tracking chart posted on the wall. *Hurricane season*. A quaint memory now, as if storms were a thing that came along within a set bound of rules and time, containable.

Rain drumming the roof, pouring over the gutters, flooding the downspouts and the streets. Land becoming sea, for a few hours, or for a day. It would pass. It would all pass. The sun would come back out and the waters would recede, for this was the only story we knew.

What a magnificent, treacherous, breathtaking moment in time we inhabit now, poised on the knife edge of foreknowledge and beauty, brevity and permanence. We know that the only thing constant is change; it is however only the more violent amplitudes of change that get our attention. Jay has an eye particularly for sunrises and sunsets—in heated skies, the best times for any pilot, much less one of a small plane, with even the workhorse engine of the Cessna 182, to fly—and for this, too, his photos possess a narrative wisdom, packaged in great beauty.

Aloft, weather is still king. Aloft, prudence is golden. The wise pilot chooses caution, moderation, responsibility. There is much that is still worth living for; there is much that is beautiful. Beloved, cherished.

On up over Caddo Lake, our largest natural freshwater lake. Farther on then, riding the edge, the slender plane buffeting on updrafts and downdrafts, as if it is not the air that is in constant pitch and turmoil, but the land below. Riding the edge and looking inward, pondering what the borders seek to contain, and what they seek to exclude. History is contained, for certain. Kemah, below, once a boardwalk to rival Coney Island's, now holds little houses like the mites between feathers on a great resting wing, ready to take flight.

This was another myth I was raised on, half a century ago, in white-bread mythological Texas: that we inhabited the edge of a frontier, a frontier that was owned by us and we alone; and that in addition to being all ours, forever and ever, it was spacious and would never run out. And that we were special, for that spaciousness, that sprawl, that emptiness.

★

Jay loves the state even more than I do. It's an honor to ride in his plane and hear him tell of his adventures. He, like me, has children sleeping back at home whom he is keen to get back to—his, within Texas's borders, and mine, beyond—but how he loves to fly, knocking out a few miles, or more than a few, each day on this grand sojourn.

We lie low in Marfa for a while as the heat coils, pulses, rises, falls. Great herds of cumulus approach from the west, drifting toward us, and suddenly the sky above fills as if with millions of bison, lightning cracking from their hooves, the sky washed clean again, and the land. Calm blue sky returns for a day, or half a day, with the scent of all things almost—intolerably fresh, if only for a little while. Something like coolness, even in summer. A moment of it, right at dusk.

I left Texas because I could not walk the land. I loved it but did not own it. I traveled west, to my public land. It occurs to me that in his own way Jay has traveled too, climbing to a sufficient height where borders, fences, boundaries, dissolve. Where they are still visible, but not nearly as meaningful, in that grappling between sky and time, as they are down on the ground.

I don't like trespassing, and I don't like having to always be hitching my leg up over barbed wire, midstride. I like to go without stopping. In the great John Graves classic, *Goodbye to a River*, he opens one chapter with a preface by Keats: "Have not all races had their first unity from a mythology, that marries them to rock and hill?"

Aloft, you can see stories not available to you below. Stories you might blunder past down at ground level. You can see how little difference there is between anything—how similar all things are, or once were, before the world began its work on the world's one-lump blockiness, its initial oneness. Up higher, you see how wind is almost no different from water, how both move in currents and waves—sandstone waves of dunes frozen in time, mid-crash: sand wind-ripples like water, then is frozen again. Time carves all elements into being: builds up, tears down, builds up, tears down. It differentiates, then conjoins.

You can see the narratives. It's a little like landing in a foreign country and finding, nonetheless, that you understand what is being said, and—important, this—how to speak. Clumps of deciduous trees upwind of a refinery, green and glowing, looking like lettuce or kale in a grand garden below, *healthy*; the refineries right next to them, trees downwind, gray and crippled, dying. The membrane between them—a chain link fence, nothing more—as invisible from the sky, in this new narrative, as it is to all the other participants in the narrative, save those who live right next to it.

Texas is oil, Texas is ag, Texas is military; Texas is water, Texas is desert. Texas is the unbearable, clotted crowdedness of nasty-ass strip malls, long troughs of them feeding the beast that is all of us. Texas is also yet, or can be, the open, empty space of a clear conscience. It's no longer so much that, really, except out here in the farthest corner. But how sweet to see a bit of it, still and yet; and what to do about that?

I have a fantasy, a dream, in which some of the large landowners of this corner of the state band together to tear down their rusting, wind-pitted, barbed-wire fences—strainers of wind and sometimes tumbleweed, nothing else; antelope limbo-wriggling beneath, then more wind, nothing else—and to allow nonmotorized public access to this larger accretion. This collective regathering; this reconnection. Places where a young person can walk for days, sky-staring. Walking toward a mountain. Walking up and over that mountain. Down the back side and onward, across the land they were born into, or came to.

This is how it was in my mind, as a young person born into Texas, and it took me a long time—eighteen years—to realize that was a myth, and to go, then, to a place, farther west, where the dream could be made real.

Dalhart—crop dusters, lined up like military squadrons, man versus soil, man versus nature. Farther on, how quickly, how crazily, the land below switches from agriculture to oil—the old swamps, old offshore point bars, mapped by our probings as a heated cake coming out of the oven is tested with toothpicks.

★

We end up killing another day in Marfa; the world is too hot. The sky is blue here, though giant pearl-white cumulus clouds are beginning to form—electrical generators, columns of almost otherworldly energy, or energy-to-come. Jay's the most conscientious—smartest—young pilot I've seen. I believe the odds are good he will become an old pilot.

"I don't want to be a statistic today," he says. The weather people are telling him we could probably fly, and he's eager to round the horn, to continue on the last leg of his journey and make it on back home, to see his family, but . . .

We visit friends of his instead, at a barbecue. I sleep in an empty mansion. The hospitality, generosity, of strangers. We awaken early, alive, to as beautiful a summer predawn as can be imagined. Stars. The world below not yet made. We fix coffee, saunter out to the airport. The lip of sun is just rising, shimmering, as we check the airplane to see how it fared in the night. No surprises. Jay's meticulous, steady. Mourning doves are calling.

We climb in, start the engine with its familiar hiss, wheeze, gasp, then throaty burbling catch of the powerful engine. Punch the rudder pedal in, pull the throttle out, swing the tail around in a one-eighty, and taxi down the empty airstrip, faster and faster, and then ascend, as if into paradise.

FOR THE LOVE
OF THE GAME

THEY COME HERE, to Brenham, from far away—from Beaumont, from Corpus, from College Station, pilgrims to their church. Maybe they were never quite good enough to cross through the gates into the kingdom of immortality, the $75 billion-plus industry of the National Football League, but they have nonetheless found a way to stay on the gridiron.

They play for the Texas Express, Brenham's semipro football team, of the Dynamic Texas Football Association, one of several semipro leagues that span the state and field a few thousand players during any given week. I came to them picturing an entire team, fifty players strong, each gloriously, foolishly, unable or unwilling to *let it go*. But it's hardly like that at all. Some of them came to take one last shot at the big time, others to prove something to themselves, or find a purpose, or escape the stresses of their days. Some of them came simply to stay out of jail.

They play in the spring rather than the fall, one of many anomalous things about the league. The term *semipro* itself is curious, a bit of a misnomer, in that it suggests that the players get paid some small amount. Not multimillion-dollar contracts, but at least a percentage of the gate, or any other receipts. There are no receipts. The players have to pay $100 to join the league, and they buy their own uniforms (metallic Kelly green with sea-foam trim, in the case of the Express).

And yet: They are not being used, or abused. They are playing on the green grass of springtime in the long shade of twilight in the heart of Texas, an hour northwest of Houston. Practice comes but once a week, around 6:00 p.m., in the center of a hundred acres of mown field, a once-upon-a-time soccer and baseball complex on the outskirts of town that now sits mostly empty ever since a new, more centrally located complex supplanted it. When the Express come to practice, this play field ringed by oaks is theirs, all theirs.

Brenham's a small entry in the league's pool; there are also teams in Houston, Austin, San Antonio, the Dallas Area, and beyond—twelve teams in all. It's late April. The season is ending soon. One game lies between the Express and a DTFA play-off berth; one practice until that game.

★

They come drifting in from the sunlight and long heat of the day, converging in the softer light of early evening and the first precious hint of cool. They are grown men, still wearing their work clothes, salt-stained from the sweat of the day. They do not come from privilege. Some work two or even three jobs. Truck drivers, security guards, septic-tank cleaners. Some are former prisoners, trying to walk the line.

Jarvis Brown is here with his girlfriend, Makayla Noah, and their new dog, a sweet young pit bull who looks like gentle Jarvis himself, who happens to be the brother of ex-Longhorn star Malcom Brown, now of the Los Angeles Rams.

Another young man drifts in, slender as a pipe cleaner and haunted-looking, like a man half looking over his shoulder, half looking ahead. (And aren't we all?) He has long dreadlocks. His name is Patrick Edwards, and he is a dead ringer for a wide receiver, with long legs and a crane-like carriage. But no, he's a quarterback.

Players' positions on the Texas Express are not identifiable by body type. Here, a man one might identify in the pros as clearly being a nose tackle—a six-foot, 305-pound mammoth of a man—turns out be the starting quarterback, Lloyd "Phat" Turner.

One of my favorite players is the oldest, David Hallback. He's thirty-nine, muscular, sports a fantastic gold tooth, wears a bandana like a pirate. He's a landscaper, digs holes, plants trees by hand. He's got a litany of nagging injuries or ailments, and as we visit he wraps athletic tape tight around various parts of himself—a wrist, a forearm, a bruised thigh. This is his seventeenth season, he says, and his last. He's been nursing a bad shoulder all year—it sounds like a torn rotator cuff—but there's nothing for that other than Advil. The only thing more difficult in his condition than tackling a ball carrier would be digging holes all day, planting trees. He says it's extra sore today, that he planted eight of them. Usually, getting six in the ground is a good day.

Only about twenty-some players show up—maybe half the team, barely enough to field a squad. More usually show up on game day, which frustrates to no end their coach, fifty-one-year-old Anthony Barnes, a garbage man by day.

As practice begins, I chat with Barnes between drills. He speaks affably with me as the players snap the ball and run their routes. Coach Barnes tells me about his own days playing semipro for the Marin Go-Devils in Northern California in the 1970s—but his eyes whip back, always, to the practice, observing and analyzing what is, and what should be. He hints at some trouble in his own life; now he's a born-again Christian.

When I ask him what's most gratifying about coaching, he says it's keeping players off the streets. "I try to get God in their lives," he tells me. "I've only lost two to the penitentiary and four to death, in nine years." When the players are short on money to get to practice, or can't buy groceries, Coach—or Kirby—will sometimes spot them some cash. More than one of the players tells me later that Coach Barnes has saved their lives.

On the field, the running backs are frisky, sensing it's quite likely they're going to be utilized heavily in Saturday's game; the forecast calls for rain. They run with confidence and creativity. The receivers don't drop their passes, though the passes are a little fluttery—the deeper they are, the more they wobble, so that as the evening goes on, they fall shorter and shorter. Arms tire. Footwork becomes less disciplined.

The shadows lengthen. Night comes. They came together for a couple of hours; they testified, rededicated, and now they are going back out into the dark. But first a prayer, all heads lowered, a huddle of young black men listening to an elder. "We could be dead!" Coach prays. "Some people didn't wake up today, didn't get up—they died! Keep a halo around us, Lord. We thank you for all those interceptions in our last game. We know that all of us are the quick and the dead. We are still alive! Help us to do your will. And help us get to practices."

★

The game. It's in a real football stadium, with a real press box—not that there is any press. That the stands are empty is a little strange, but not as much as you'd think. The field is what matters. It's just a high school stadium, Cedar Park High, in a northern Austin suburb, but at a big school in Texas, that's pretty similar to the college stadiums I remember from Utah and Idaho in the 1970s.

Toussam, from Cameroon, is suited up entirely, looking sharp and ready to go, while other players sit in the bleachers and on benches in various states of readiness . . . A few stretch, but for the most part the players scramble for little bits and pieces—a buckle for a helmet, a mouthguard, a missing glove—deep in the reaches of their duffels. They don't have access to the locker rooms here, so they are living out of their bags.

The kickoff, the most dangerous moment in any game, has all the ritualistic tension you'd feel in an NFL stadium. There's the run-up, the kick, the ball spinning through the air, and everyone running full tilt, as if storming the beaches, toward an inevitable violent collision. The Express receive; the returner breaks to the outside, puts on a little puff of speed, but then is tripped up.

The game batters and slugs back and forth. No one dominates. At times it brings to mind a gun firing blanks—the ball is snapped, the hammer drops and strikes the firing pin, but no bullet comes out. Not like the pros. And how could it be?

Even Lloyd "Phat" Turner has trouble. He looks like Gulliver amid the Lilliputians, but the defenders from Cedar Park—the Punishers—bring him down with one-on-one attempts. He is hurried, indecisive. And the offensive line is leaking. Cedar Park sacks Turner three times in a row.

On defense, however, David Hallback is a dervish. He, most among them, looks like a pro—fending off blockers, throwing them aside, reading the runner, squaring up to the runner's numbers, lowering his hurt shoulder, and popping them so hard you can hear the plastic-on-plastic smack.

Patrick Edwards goes in for Turner and runs a few sweeps, pitches and flash-screens to the wide receivers, to get the ball out of that ferocious pressure coming from up the middle, and starts to move the ball down the field. Brenham scores but misses the extra point.

Hallback, who has been single-handedly shutting down the right side of the offense—stripping the ball from carriers, knifing through blockers—continues to impose his will. He plays at such a higher level than anyone around him that Cedar Park begins double- and sometimes even triple-teaming him. Blocking him in the back. They've got to do something. He's still slipping out of their holds and pulling down the runners.

After one play in which a runner finally gets around the edge and scoots just past him, Hallback loses his cool. He leaps up, waves his arms, howls at the ref—where are the flags? All the way across the field, I see his gold tooth flashing like semaphore, and the Cedar Park players, having regained some vestige of control, appear delighted. Suddenly Hallback is in their midst, trying to confront one or another of them, and a yellow flag launches like a flare from one of the refs. Coach Barnes, who is about nothing if not control and discipline, now loses *his* cool, goes charging out onto the field to summon Hallback away from the scrum.

Coach puts his big hand on Hallback's shoulder and then wraps both arms around him—a bear hug of restraint—so that for a second it seems like he's tackling the player. "He was blocking me in the *back*," Hallback says, sounding as heartbroken as a five-year-old—*it isn't fair*—and Coach has to walk him farther away from the field, away from the sidelines, out to the cinder track that encircles the stadium.

The game proceeds, uncaring for the personal drama at its perimeter. Without their star safety, the Express move in reverse. The Punishers advance the ball, and soon enough they're across the goal line, which sets off a new round of lamentations by Hallback, who has returned to the sideline. Some players move away from him, while others try to console him. If the Express don't win a play-off berth, this could be the last game of Hallback's life.

Brenham gets the ball back, and Patrick puts together a little drive that turns into a big drive when, on third and long, they convert on a pass play. Now the running backs start to take control of the game, ripping off six and then ten and twelve yards at a time. The offensive linemen keep up their run-blocking, if not yet stopping the pass rush. The Express score a touchdown.

Now it's the defense's turn to stop Cedar Park, and—not yet with forgiveness but with a weary utility—Coach nods that Hallback can go back out onto the field. He fumbles with his helmet, pulls it on quickly, bolts from the bench, runs out across the field— not like the extraordinarily fit man he is, looking over the fence at the nearing territory of middle age, but instead like a boy, running out to join his teammates.

Cedar Park has far fewer players than Brenham does—fewer reserves—and by the fourth quarter, they're wearing down. Part of it might also be that, after three quarters of practice, the Express are starting to come together. They send Jarvis Brown up the middle again and again, devouring the clock. They win the game. They've made the play-offs.

★

Afterward, Coach speaks to the team. Everyone stands in a circle midfield. "We got *lucky*," Coach says. Tough love is his job, and it's why the players keep coming back to him—to be bridled, to be directed. To be coached. To be given a place where they can protect—protect the ball, protect the quarterback, protect the lead, protect the clock—but also to be protected. They are safe here. They know the rules; they have a hand in the outcome.

Still, they want good times, too. They came here to play. To remember the basics of running and jumping, leaping and diving, tumbling and rolling. To get up and run again and to be with each other, briefly, and finally, as a team.

"Gentlemen," Coach says, "the Ugly Thing reared its head again. The Ugly Thing came into our midst again, and we did not strike it down. I will not say its name." The huddle is utterly silent, and I can hear every player breathing. "If we are to get better, we must not let the Ugly Thing come into our presence and have its way with us again."

Perhaps for him the Ugly Thing is them not showing up for practice, them not being perfect. He wants to be able to mold and shape them, but how can he work with what isn't there? Coach falls silent, but the players are still listening, no doubt considering whatever the Ugly Thing is for each of them. It does not matter that they will not advance beyond the first round of the play-offs. Nothing matters except right now; they were flawed, but were delivered a victory nonetheless.

There is no one in the stands, and the Cedar Park team has already packed up and left. The springtime humidity is building, and not-so-distant lightning cleaves the now-black sky. A mist begins to fall, sheets and waves of it drifting past the high halogen lights and cooling us all. The players run back to the sidelines to gather their gear, then run for their cars and trucks, laughing and calling out to one another in the night in some combination of joy and relief.

That's the thing about football, or one of the things—whether pro, semipro, or any variety. Sometimes, for a fleeting moment, it can be perfect. Complicated and perfect. And how lovely to glimpse such a dream.

WHEN A HUNTER DIES

IT'S TOO CLOSE TO THE BONE; this is not the way it's supposed to go. Always before, our hunters have left quietly, in perfect chronology, as orderly as children filing out to playground recess, one at a time, each successive oldest passing through that door—as if leaving the camp house to go look around for something, one more hunt—and then not coming back. Stepping through that door and into the landscape of our memory. Old Howard—not blood-related, but the man who owned, and leased to us, the deer pasture, stepping out quietly in his late eighties; and then Old Granddaddy, a while later, also in his late eighties. When it was his time.

The next two oldest, Uncle Jimmy and my dad, Charlie, began showing hints of mortality in their seventies—Uncle Jimmy, with a stroke, and Dad, with bladder and then prostate cancer ten years ago, but both battling those things back, recovering, and still hunting, hunting on, and still with us.

My oldest cousin wasn't supposed to step to the head of the line, wasn't supposed to cut in front of anyone. The oldest son of Uncle Jimmy, as I am Charlie's oldest, he and I (his name was Rick, too) were supposed to become the Old Ones someday. That was the model that had been presented to us; that was what we knew. The assumption if not outright assurance that that was how it would be.

It's true that Rick was already in his sixties. It's true also that in my mind he is still a handsome, reckless teenager, burning with life; that he is still young and daring charismatic, troubled. Did I say reckless? It's true that in my mind he and I are both still young and vital, undiminished, uncompromised.

★

Like all of us who have been gathering here once a year to hunt for a week—uncles, cousins, brothers, grandfather, nephews—the deer pasture is, was, his church. He was religious—he differed from me there; he was a minister—but he had this other church, too, as do we all. We're old enough now that we have children who wander it, who hunt it, in that one week each year, the first week of November. There are more bunk beds in the camp house now, more hunters, but no matter: the juniper of the thousand acres, for the most part, hides us, as it hides the deer.

But we see things, if not always each other, as we walk along the stony-bottomed creeks, and pass between the rounded boulders, and sit quietly beneath the oaks, hiding in a rampart of broken limbs, remnants of where the old trees' branches broke off, burdened by their own sweeping weight, their own excessive reach.

We sit beneath such trees, motionless, hidden from the world in our camouflage, and watch raccoons trundle past, bobcats, armadillo, turkeys, and, always, deer.

I grew up with him; I knew him for all of my fifty-seven years, and I hunted with him thirty-five of those years, for one week each year, without fail. Thirty-five weeks, day and night, cleaning deer, cooking, doing the dishes, telling stories, fixing (or not fixing) broken trucks, broken water pumps, nailing tin back on the roof after thunderstorms, listening to Louisiana State University and University of Texas football games, to Dallas Cowboy and Houston Oiler football games. Thirty-five weeks—just a bit shy of a full year of deer hunting with him, three-hundred-sixty-five days and nights, though always at the same time of year, so that in some ways it would, and did, seem that time remained frozen, until it wasn't, and it didn't.

By all rights, we should have had a full year.

★

As he grew older, he slept later and later. It became less and less a concern to him that he find a deer. He talked a big game—pretended to be always on the lookout for "Ol' Mossy Horns"—but as the years went on, he loved that bed. We'd have a campfire in the evenings, watch the stars, and the flat-topped silhouette of Hudson Mountain to the east—always, shooting stars in that country. One night, long ago, one passed so close to us that Randy and I heard its ripping crackle, smelled its scorch—an amazement—and then, one by one, we'd drift back into the bunkhouse, lie down on our bunks, and read. He'd fall asleep with the book on his chest and, later, begin snoring. It was always a race with all of us to see who could be the first to get to sleep, for that reason. He didn't do anything halfway.

He'd had tragedy in his life. A car wreck in which his wife was killed. Another accident in which a jacked-up truck he was working on fell on his hand, crushing it. He was a doctor and a surgeon; he couldn't practice after that, but he volunteered abroad for weeks each year. Another year or more of his life, I suppose, in the cumulative, spent doing that.

But about the deer hunting. As young men—boys, really—this thousand acres of hill country hardscrabble was to us a wild garden, a land of rattlesnakes, cactus, wild pigs, and giant granite boulders shaped by time into fantastic hoodoo forms: a clenched fist, an Easter Island visage, a rhinoceros, a hippo. We hiked up and down the water-smoothed slot canyons, swam in the deepest pools beneath sparkling waterfalls. From the first day, it was our heaven; the place which, when we were away from it, we were always working our way back to.

He was a man of enormous passions and appetites, which can be, of course, a precursor, a way of segueing into the fact that at different times of his life he had problems with the bottle.

Demons, I guess you could say. Actually I guess it was always a struggle, and he was either winning or losing. The last years of his life he was winning, and I'm glad for that. I'm grateful I have no such challenges, grateful I don't have to waste days, then years, owned by such a disease, and can instead—through the fluke of luck—sit quietly in the junipers, and in the oak creek bottoms, and listen to, and watch, the trickling, gurgling plates of gold water swirl past, fractals of gleaming water spinning; disassembling, reassembling.

This last year—the last year we had him, it turned out—I was sitting in the deep shade, the abiding shade, on a wicked-hot day (gone, it seems, are the crisp November hunts of my youth) and as I watched, a male wood duck came drifting down that lane of gold light, his plumage wildly flamboyant, charismatic, outrageous; and yet, he, too, was seeking shade.

I do not look forward to the gap of him this year. Those hoary clichés that we try to stand on, like a foundation, at such times: *He will be missed. It won't be the same without him.*

No, it won't.

★

Here are places we can go to find him, now that he has stepped across and gone to where the others have gone, gone on ahead.

The Water Gap. There's a tradition, each night-before—especially the first night-before—where we think and talk about where we each want to go the next morning. He loved the East Side, the Back Side, and the Burned-Off Hill. But always the Water Gap, and Turkey Hollow, also called Panther Hollow back in the old days. A narrow cleft, a deep dark place, spooky, yet so beautiful; and spookiest of all, and most beautiful, right at dusk, with darkness coming in over darkness. The arching limbs of hickory trees forming a canopy over that steep canyon, both sides of the hollow so steep that it is hard to stand up straight, easy to tumble and roll to the bottom. A good place to sit quietly and watch, wait. Of course he loved it, and we knew on the nights that he got back into camp a little late that that was where he had been hunting, sitting there in the gathering gloom, and then beyond (waiting all the way until the last light before coming the long way home, the long way back).

Like I said, as he grew older, he always slept late. It makes no sense that for once he should be the first among us—among the cousins and brothers—to head out. It's so atypical. It's so surprising. I forget sometimes that's why it's called life.

The *how* does and does not matter. He was on a motorcycle— *You're too old*, I want to tell him, and, to be honest, with some anger, or at least irritation—but it must also be said it wasn't his fault. It is also true people don't see motorcycles unless they are looking for them.

The last time I saw him was at my youngest brother's wedding, in Austin, at the first edge of spring. So it goes.

★

He always came into camp with stories. Sometimes, being dramatic, I think he embellished the facts. He put ornate curlicues on them, elaborate punctuations, burnished. So much so that on the rare occasion—or I assume it was rare—he came back in with one incredible story or another, one which was unadorned, and we didn't believe it; he would be surprised, frustrated. No, *really*, he'd say. God's honest truth!

Such was the story of his sighting of a mountain lion one morning, over on the East Side.

No one believed him, of course. And to this day, I do not know yet whether he did or not. When he described with admirable specificity its acorn-gold color and long tail floating behind it, we razzed him that he had just seen an extraordinarily large fox squirrel, one with an exceptionally bushy tail.

I for one always believed him, though I never gave him the pleasure of acknowledging that—how I wish I had, now—and I even went so far as to make lion tracks with my fist, my palm, in a sand creek to spur the rumor and get him agitated. *See, I told you!* he said, coming back into camp, wanting to show us all the tracks he'd found.

For twenty years, he continued to insist the sighting was legit, carrying on each year, telling us to be careful, that there were lions out there.

I for one believe he saw the lion, and it must have been an amazing thing. A thing that scared him, and filled him with the awe of the world's beauty and the way that something surprising, something wonderful, can happen in any next-step. And that he carried that with him, the way we all carry certain things—gains and losses, regrets and hopes—with us, all of the days, across all terrain.

★

Oh yes, another thing: he was a father. The most important thing. He had been a husband, at different times, and tried his best; a son, brother, cousin, nephew, grandson, ditto—but he was a father. I know for a fact that on his rambles through this land of granite—old igneous fire cooled to stones that grew rounded over time and glittered crystalline with the beauty locked within, the boulders slowly crumbling and dissolving over time, so that those sparkling, diamond-like crystals spill loose and spread across the ground—that that was what he was proudest of: being a father. He was always talking about his children, updating us with their doings—four daughters and a son.

I know for a fact that in his quiet times he would be looking around at the beauty of the place, and he would be considering not his travails and stresses, his troubles and challenges, but his blessings; that here, if only here, all worries became diminished, put in their proper, tiny, mortal perspective.

Sometimes, deer would walk right past him while he was thinking such things.

We all, always, want one more day; and if given that extra day, what would we do with it? Not, I think, go hunting; not, I think, focus on the killing of yet one more deer.

Which is precisely what makes those days—uncounted, and timeless—so very valuable. Who knows when the last hunt is? Rarely does anyone know. Whether this is a blessing or not, I cannot say, only that we were in no way ready for him to leave without coming back, and that we will be talking about him, telling stories about him, for a long time yet to come, as he told stories about those, the Old Ones, who had been here before us. He has become one of them, already. Already, so soon.

MAPS

I NEVER DREAM ABOUT MAPS. I used to draw them for a living. I have dreams about every other passion. It occurs to me that to dream about maps might be almost impossible—like dreaming about dreaming. Mapping is its own activity, its own universe, separate from the rest of the living. One is already in the dream.

I'm not sure when I first learned to see the world through the veinous overlay of maps. It would have started in Texas, where I grew up—born in Fort Worth, living briefly in Odessa, then growing up in Houston. The first labor for which I was paid involved maps. My father is a geophysicist, an interpreter of seismic data gotten from thumper trucks and jug lines, where customized heavy trucks send sound waves cascading down into the earth through either a concussive slamming of the earth's surface with a specialized plate, or with charges of dynamite dropped into shallow drill holes.

The waves travel straight down, slowing the farther they get from the source. Measuring the web of sound that returns to the surface, then—counting the seconds it takes the sound reflection to bounce back upward—allows the dreamer the opportunity to imagine better the nature of what lies below: thick, sound-muffling porous formations, or brittle, thin, tight seams that could trap the ascent of hydrocarbons. Freshwater, saltwater, oil, gas, stone—an infinitude of horizons lie below, as close to being frozen in time as is possible. Each horizon can be as thin as the skin of the earth on which we stand, the surface of this earth its own one data point in this instant, and we, drill holes into which the charge has been dropped.

It amazes me, remembering some of those deep elevator dives—hurtling downward through the Paleozoic, past the Devonian and even Ordovician, all the way down to the Cambrian and sometimes even pre-Cambrian—that we ever made it back up to the surface.

Later, computer programs were created to make the maps we used to build in our minds—mapping the underground architecture of the unseen, as if entering Atlantis's lost lands, civilizations of stone and swamp. Now infallible printers scribe colorful lines onto the maps in 3-D relief, where decades earlier we drew contour maps by hand, our maps replete with the sweeping arc of faults, both upthrown and downthrown, thrust and shear and reverse and normal faults, as well as unconformities—places underground where an entire formation has disappeared due to faulting or differential erosion.

In the unconformities, all traces of the preceding physical world have been swept away. Mountain ranges have been worn smooth and washed away completely, carried off to sea, where the individual grains of the disassembled then begin their slow patient process of reformation; hiding once again, with a complete new identity, so that which existed before, both the time and the place, is made into something even less than a dream.

Before the computers arrived, it was not an algebraic or even a geometric process by which we parsed the messages from below, the sound waves returning to the surface like homing pigeons coming back home in waves with a flurry of feathers. Instead, there was calculus involved, interpretation, intuition. It took a cavernous mind to read and know and consider all the variables that could affect the speed and character of the bounce back.

How darkly they imprinted themselves on the paper scrolling through the feedback machines, every tremor and squiggle more nuanced than the same ink needle's wavering response in reading the activity of the human heart, or the electrical fields, the storms and lulls, streaks and surges, of the brain itself. As if far below lay the earth's sleeping brain, sealed in stone, sheathed with innumerable layers of time, and with that brain bathed in the oils and vapors of old Paleozoic swamps—all the living that had gone away or moved on.

The machine that recorded the returning echoes had a needle, like the stylus on a phonograph, that transcribed this different language of sound, this different language of the memory and density of stones. The needle warbled and wobbled as if taking wild dictation.

The scribble of the needle, the record of the jarring collision, like the cursive and still elegant but eventually trembling script my grandmother would use in addressing her letters to me, even into her nineties—a tremble that seemed to speak not of diminishment but passion. As if the entire world was vibrating at its core, and she could feel it now; it had found her and she alone among all my other correspondents had found it, the source of that trembling.

When my father had the secret scripts in hand—long coils of paper only a few inches wide but twenty feet long, or longer (reminiscent in the limitless spools that I would later learn were the way Jack Kerouac wrote, or typed), my father would, with colored pencils, correlate one shot-point's vertical revelations to those gathered from the next shot-point: the place where the thumper truck or jug lines had been set, and so on.

He colored the representations of the various strata different colors, then lay the two scripts together, each long vertical spooling of paper recording the sonic innards of a borehole. He placed several of the logs side by side on his desk, moving one up and another down, adjusting his coded colors like puzzle pieces until the picture became clear, and whether of a fractured earth or a whole earth below, no matter; what mattered was where the oil could be hiding. He calculated depths, distances, slopes. He could tell which strata were the ones most likely to hold oil or gas. He knew what he was hunting.

It was my job, however, after he had made those interpretations, to erase his color codings with an electric eraser. I had to be careful not to let the whirring eraser tip linger too long or rub too deep, or it would burn a hole in the paper—but I needed to erase the codings so he could start over, or use the logs again whenever new data was received. It was not unlike the process, I realize, by which I write stories and novels, dozens of drafts—sanding, erasing, recalibrating; tying one character to another, one character to a place, and to each other, with things shifting, always.

The sweet smell of eraser filings, the heat of friction, filled the room. The whirring of the eraser lulled my mind into a kind of hypnosis, until I felt I too was diving down into the crypt of time, my hand not writing the script of underground, but erasing proof that it was down there—undoing each ledge and shelf. Making it be as if it had never been down there.

I understood from an early age there was a significant disparity between what one saw in the world above, in Texas—the long sightlines in the salt flats and scrublands around Midland; the tiny hills and subtle swellings—and all the world below, which seemed constructed of nothing but verticality: jagged extrusions, dikes, sills, and encased, perhaps not permanently but more so than that above, which was still exposed to the furies of erosion. The fact that one could see more up at the surface only spurred one to imagine the opposite. At that young age, I, like so many others, would read from Antoine de Saint-Exupéry, "The airplane has unveiled for us the true face of the Earth. For centuries, highways had been deceiving us."

I had begun rambling the undeveloped old hardwood forests in the floodplain along the Buffalo Bayou after school, out toward the Katy Prairie—what we would now probably call urban wilderness but which back then was just woods—and the verticality of the eraser work, down, ever down, had to it the same quality of my lateral jungle ramblings in which I followed the script of the wandering chocolate-milk bayou and looked for shallow places or fallen logs on which I could cross to the other side.

My father's maps lay draped over all four corners of his giant work desk, which had been an operating table in the Civil War, made of walnut, knife-notched, and darkened with the stain of the spilled inkwells of his craft, and looking like the blood that surely must have been spilled on the table before being wiped clean. The table held the memory of trauma, perhaps, as a violin or guitar is said to resonate almost forever with the music that has emanated from it, over time. It was familiar to me—I did my homework there after school each day—but I could feel a darkness within it.

★

It was Texas. In the 1970s I played football—it was Texas—and became for whatever reasons fascinated with the gears of logic within football. I sketched plays in my school notebooks, slants and stunts and twists, all manners of intricate blocking schemes designed to free one of a multiplicity of runners from out of the backfield—this was the era of the wishbone formation, the quarterback triple-option (today's simpler version is the zone read)—and it made so much sense to me then, and still does. *Get the ball down the field; run to set up the pass and pass to set up the run.*

There was to football an ever-changing sinuosity of logic, and a duality: one thing cannot succeed or even exist without the other thing, its opposite. I realize now I was building a writer's mind just as much as I had been with the early earth-diving. The routes one ran as a receiver, or between tacklers, with passion, were but contours on a map.

I went to college in Utah—played a little football, skied a lot—and as a novice skier learned to read fall lines, carving contours through the snow, tracks that would be gone the next day, or soon buried beneath that same day's snow. I then moved to Mississippi where I, too, worked as a geologist, making maps with little more than a handful of clues—some old drill cuttings, some core data from an old well log—searching, tracking down the quarry that sought to hide in the highest reaches of underground anticlines, some little larger than the dome of the capital in Jackson where I lived for several years. And in this searching, groping, probing, reaching for the unknown, searching with deep desire and intensity, I was continuing to build a writer's brain, mapping a landscape in my brain through which a writer's thoughts and passions could wander.

I missed the West, however—its long horizon and big sky, of which there was so much that it was possible to confuse space as a kind of time, and even an excess of time.

I was still mapping—consulting, drafting prospects, searching for investors. It was the early 1980s. Bill McKibben's *The End of Nature* would not come out until 1989. We all thought natural gas was good, that it displaced coal. Gas, and its cleaner-burning fume, was invisible.

★

I, like everyone then, drew my maps by hand. The sweeps and curls and curves of my maps still flowed from my mind down through my neck and into my chest and shoulders down through and around my forearm and wrist, through my hand and then out of my fingers with which I held, sometimes softly and other times with greater tension, the HB #2 pencil as it transformed the blank white linen space on the map into a curling narrative, the pencil chasing the truth underground.

I was still mapping, but I had begun to write. The landscape in my head had been cultivated, and—luck, happenstance—I found a bookstore in Jackson, Mississippi: Lemuria, named for the subaqueous antediluvian land of Atlantis, and, a short time later, Square Books in Oxford. The proprietors hand-sold me dozens, then hundreds of books—Southern literature, nature writing, Russian literature, and, falling like rain, the richness of the blossoming American short-story renaissance into which I had awakened.

I sat dream-fixed as if in a low-tide mudflat, listening to the screaming of seagulls, books raining down upon me, barefooted, pants cuffs rolled up to stay out of the muck; but I was in the muck, and all I had to do was pick up any book I could reach during that time and read, and the tide just kept on going out, exposing more and more treasures and bounty. I wandered the strandline of that time, plucking and picking what I wanted, listening to the surf, walking and reading—the journey of those readings its own kind of contour line. As would be the sentences I began to write, slowly at first though with no concern or consideration of failure any more than would a walker along the coast in Mexico, stopping to pick up the pearl of pinwheels or cones of whelk, consider the idea of success or failure in so simple and pleasing a gesture, and then a life, spent beachcombing.

★

I began to hunt. I did not carry a GPS. It is so important for the traveler, the cartographer, to become lost. It sounds horribly facile to say it this way, but it is no less true for that. If you do not get lost you cannot know what it feels like to be found, or to find one's way out. The times I have become lost are the times when I have often found what I am most searching for, or most desire.

As did football, the escape routes of elk make a real and certain sense to me. The maps of their days are acutely calibrated to survival, to the continuation of the condition of life.

What might any of our own lives look like—our daily movements and gestures—if we did not occupy the softer place of
sprawl we now inhabit, where choices seem muddled and perhaps
worst of all, insignificant, unimportant, but instead lived all our
hours with the incandescence of the hunt?

It is not enough that the elk seek rest, bedding in deep thickets no other traveler can penetrate without a violence of cracking
limbs and branches. It is not enough that they "sleep"—*rest*—with
their backs to the wind, able to smell anything approaching from
that 180-degree upwind vector, and that their faces—with eyes on
either side of their head, in the ocular positioning of prey—are
able to see 180 degrees downwind, their zone of vulnerability.

With their four hooves and their nearly constant motion,
readjusting ever so slightly to the most minute changes in wind
currents, they scribe and reposition like 750-pound barometers.
They bed beside ledges so if something does somehow sneak in
on them from downwind, they can, in their sudden startlement,
simply vault over the ledge or cliff and disappear—their immense
antlers thrashing for a split second in the brush and thicket, then
gone: a dream, save for the rank sweet scent of them, and the
elk-shaped ice shell of where they had been sleeping in the snow.

It is very hard to catch up and connect with them as a hunter—
one must learn, over the course of a lifetime, that which has been
mapped into their blood by a million years of success. And when
one is fortunate enough to intersect their travels—to know where
they are going, and why, and how to get there just in the same
moment that they do—is delicious, as mentally stimulating as it
is physically grueling. It quickly becomes an addiction, and aging
knees, and the waning of hunt lust, only tempers the addiction,
never erases it entirely.

And in the maps one studies each night, exhausted from the
day's rambles yet planning already the next dawn's—there is the
utter freedom of immersion, and of flight, for you have been

incorporated into, and sustained by, a world so much older that it predates even the time of humans. It is simple and complicated and brutal and, as with all life, laced with generous dollops of luck.

Doug Peacock says hunting is the act that has most developed the organic intelligence that defines our species—that it is so much more foundational than farming. I believe it, and I like to imagine the rapidity of the first blossoming in our minds as we made plans, strategies, tactics, and then tools for hunting. Paradoxically, perhaps communal or solitary hunting, as much as anything, gave rise to the condition of or space in our minds for empathy. By knowing, learning, understanding, of primal necessity, how another species lived, in every hour of every season—what its needs were, its fears, its strengths and vulnerabilities—we became more deeply wedded to it. That knowledge would continue to be exploited for survival and sustenance, but once the synapses and neural pathways all linked up, it was all but impossible to not simultaneously possess empathy.

I remember being a young hunter, not quite knowing what I was doing. I remember also feeling all the connections finally attach to one another, the myriad branchings and curlicue meanderings that for a long time were but beautiful culs-de-sac, images and observations not yet connected to all other things: the dampness of the soil in a certain grove of trees, larkspur satin-purple amid a south-facing slope of talus, the gnawed stripes on a short thigh bone found moldering beneath cedars. At first, all of it meant nothing, and then, one day, all of it meant everything. I was suddenly fluent. I suddenly understood my prey. And from that—from the land, and from one's quarry, one's desire, one's need—came religion.

★

Why do you write? someone asked Flannery O'Connor, and—one senses she was irritated by so personal a question; why does one choose to serve any god or God?—she simply said (snapped, I hope), *Because I'm good at it.* Next question.

Others have modified the answer when asked that question or similar ones. They speak of their desire to write the kind of stories they themselves would like to read; and for me, as I recall, that was more of the generative impulse. And it seems later in life to have returned to me. Not an original observation, not by a long shot, but in the way that all contours must close on themselves to contain the mapped element, my sentences seek once again to tell stories I wish I could read or experience. Where as a young man the stories I wrote had a kind of pyrotechnical yearning for . . . well, for what, I'm still not sure—an expansion of borders and boundaries, I'd guess, not so much a mythical realm at all as instead an exploration of the possible rather than simply the probable—my stories now are more imagistic. I try to keep the tension and pyrotechnics beneath the surface. I remain fascinated by the disparity between above and below.

★

Nearly forty years later I find myself for the first time in my lengthening not nurtured by a map, but bedeviled, drained. As if a fault or fracture has occurred in my artistic body and a great treasure house of essence is flowing out—a thing vital, which I wish to contain, like water. More is going out than is coming in.

The valley where I now live in northwestern Montana, and where I have lived for thirty-four years, has the most endangered subpopulation of grizzlies in the state. Only twenty-five remain here in the Yaak.

The Yaak is a different valley from the rest of the rock- and icescapes of western Montana. It's also the state's the lowest elevation and the wettest, moist biological diverse valley. It's also the most northernmost—a sanctuary, a climate refuge, against the dragon breath of global warming.

A recreational through-hikers' club, the Pacific Northwest Trail Association, envisioned a straight line conjoining the high-volume and immensely popular Pacific Crest Trail to the high-volume Continental Divide Trail. Designed as a spur to accept overflow from those other two trails, the proposed Pacific Northwest Trail (PNT) was rejected by the US Forest Service and US Fish and Wildlife Service for thirty-two years. The agencies cited first and foremost the deleterious impacts on the endangered Yaak grizzly bears.

Nonetheless, in 2009, the hikers' club, based out of Washington state, convinced their delegation to introduce a single paragraph to a must-pass federal omnibus bill, codifying the trail straight through Montana public lands previously designated as core territory dedicated to the recovery of those few Yaak grizzlies. (Currently there are thought to be only three or four breeding-age females with cubs. Grizzly bears are the second-slowest reproducing land mammal in North America.)

The hikers' club favors hopping from high peak to high peak. Unfortunately, there are only a very few high peaks in the Yaak, and it is these remote alpine meadows that the female grizzlies with their young depend on most, in summer and fall. Often the Yaak's alpine meadows are little larger than a suburban lawn. Study after study shows that pedestrians—whether well-intentioned or not—cause stress upon grizzlies when entering their core habitat, displacing them roughly one thousand feet to either side of a trail. In the Yaak's tiny meadows, this results in a complete "taking" of the meadows by the hikers.

A map can be deadly. A map can be powerful. A map can destroy a million years of crafted beauty. It's easy to forget, lost in the mystery of maps, that not all maps lead to wonder, awe, art, or discovery.

What's particularly galling on the PNT route is that forty years ago, legendary grizzly biologist Chuck Jonkel—who was one of many scientists opposing the hikers' club route—went to the trouble to craft a hiker-friendly map that went to even more high peaks, south of the Kootenai River, but avoided the fat middle of core grizzly habitat, and which gave through-hikers the opportunity, if they chose, to re-provision in the small trail towns of Libby and Troy.

There is no evidence in the Congressional record that the hikers' club divulged Dr. Jonkel's map to the committee that signed off on the omnibus bill—hundreds of pages of omnibus minutiae with that one damning trail paragraph hidden within—and it became law.

So now, we seek sponsorship of another piece of legislation that will reroute the trail to a scenic alternative. Or, if that is not amenable, to simply not have a PNT in Montana. Hercules bending iron bars did not face a more daunting task.

After forty years of failure, the hikers' club appears more interested in "preserving" their legislative paragraph than in the fate of the Yaak's last grizzlies. Our group has published a map that shows hikers the ethical southern route. Waiting for Congress to act these days feels distressingly similar to waiting for the world to end. We aren't going to wait. For many of us, the grizzly is nothing less than a religion. Fighting for it is therefore a holy act. As the last wild grizzlies in the little Yaak valley wander those spines—perhaps looking over their shoulders to see now what packtrain of humans might be coming into their small living spaces—they deserve to not have to step aside, and away from those little high-altitude meadows, to make way for the coming streams of targeted, concentrated recreation.

Unlike the through-hikers, the bears possess no other contours to follow to get where they are going; this is their home, and this is all there is for them. Will they blink out, a race of bears made extinct by the desires of recreation? Only time, the great revealer, will tell.

I don't write much fiction these days. There is a cruel red line laid down just beneath the Canadian border and my days and nights now are spent trying to erase it, to bend it south—to birth a new, better map. To preserve the habitat of beauty, and of a thing I love fiercely. It is all the same, a life. Only the scenery changes. All will be buried or washed away. And yet.

ACKNOWLEDGMENTS

The author is grateful to the following publications, in which some of the essays collected here have previously appeared.

The Learned Pig: "Maps"
Esquire: "A Dog in the Hand"
Field & Stream: "When a Hunter Dies"
Garden & Gun: "Into the Woods with James McMurtry: Hunting Wild Turkeys, Great Songs, and Wide Open Spaces," "Toledo Bend," and "Writing in Stone"
Adventures with a Texas Naturalist, by Roy Bedichek (Austin: UT Press, 1994): "Adventures with a Texas Naturalist: Roy Bedichek" (published as introduction)
Texas Monthly: "3,822 Miles," "For the Love of the Game," and "Into the Wild"
Texas Parks & Wildlife: "The Farm" and "The Shining Marsh"
Wildsam Field Guides: The Moon, edited by Taylor Bruce (n.p.: Wildsam, 2019): "Moon Story"
Men's Journal: "Into the Fire"